SITUATION NORMAL A.F.U.

SITUATION NORMAL A.F.U.

A FLATFOOTED SOLDIER TELLS ALL

by

Oscar R. Nordstrom

Situation Normal —A. F. U.: A Flatfooted Soldier Tells All
Softcover Edition Copyright © 2020 by Oscar R. Nordstrom
All rights reserved.

No part of this book may be reproduced in any form or by any means, electronic or mechanical, except by a reviewer who may quote brief passages in a review to be printed in a magazine, newspaper, or on the Internet – without permission in writing from the publisher.

This is a work of nonfiction. While all the events depicted in this book are true, names have been changed to protect the privacy of the people involved. The conversations in the book all come from the author's recollections and do not represent a word-for-word transcript. Rather, the author has retold them in a way that evokes the feeling and meaning what was said and, in all instances, accurately reflects the essence of the actual dialogue.

Publication date: April, 2020
Softcover Edition
ISBN: 978-0-9983109-5-4

Library of Congress Control Number: 2020907960

Manufactured in the United States of America

10 9 8 7 6 5 4 3

Interior and Cover Design by John Clifton, Foley Square Books
info@foleysquarebooks.com

Cover illustration by Daniel Leister
danielleister.com

North Stream Publishing • 36 Thiells Mt. Ivy Rd.
Pomona, NY 10970

EMAIL: *info@northstreampublishing.com*
www.northstreampublishing.com

There Are Three Ways to Do Things —

The Right Way

The Wrong Way

The Army Way

...Old Army Axiom

Contents

Acknowledgements 12

Introduction 12

CHAPTER 1

What did I step into? 15

CHAPTER 2

From White Hall Street to halfway round the world 19

CHAPTER 3

The "Ultimate Warrior" 26

CHAPTER 4

Survey dates back to Ancient Egyptians—admirable! 49

CHAPTER 5

Ocean voyages— not all they're cracked up to be 65

CHAPTER 6

Elvis Presley slept here (?) 69

CHAPTER 7

Fast Cars, Howitzers, and the Black Market. 74

CHAPTER 8

Pitching woo—instead of a tent 85

CHAPTER 9

Germany's answer to St. Patrick's Day and *Mardi Gras* 97

CHAPTER 10

Changing gears without a clutch 100

CHAPTER 11

Showing my stuff— and nearly getting kicked out on my ass 105

CHAPTER 12

Did anyone say – Animal House?? 111

CHAPTER 13

Under Water... 117

CHAPTER 14

Dancing to *Bésame Mucho* and Article 15's................................. 121

CHAPTER 15

The stuff that legends are made of 128

CHAPTER 16

No time for Sergeants—or MP's, for that matter 141

CHAPTER 17

A new winter Olympic sport... 148

CHAPTER 18

Typing with two fingers and a bum shoulder................................ 151

CHAPTER 19

A Hallowed Army Tradition 156

CHAPTER 20

Auf Weidersehen 159

POSTSCRIPT 162

ABOUT THE AUTHOR 162

ARMY TERMS, ACRONYMS AND SLANG USED IN THIS BOOK 164

PHOTOS 167

Acknowledgements

For their gracious help and support, I'd like to express my gratitude to John Clifton of Foley Square Books, Daniel Leister (illustrator), and especially to my Army buddies Donald ("Rusty") Rush, Robert ("Merch") Merchant, and all the other guys I had the honor to serve with. Most of all, I'd like to thank my late wife Susan Nee Fay, for inspiring me to be a better man (to borrow a Jack Nicholson line from the movie *As Good as It Gets*). Susan's grace and beautiful soul were a gift to her family and all who knew her.

Introduction

The events about to unfold in this book occurred over 50 years ago, during what was then America's most unpopular war. You may ask why I waited so long to write a story about my time in the service, which started with my enlistment in August of 1965. Certainly, the statute of limitations for any offenses I might have committed has long since been rendered unenforceable. And since this book was written as a comedy, you may wonder what was so funny about being in the Army at the height of the war in Viet Nam.

Before getting to that answer, it's necessary to mention why I enlisted in the Army in the first place. The answer lies, in part, in my wanting to follow in the footsteps of my two older and revered brothers, who had enlisted in the Navy. So why did I enlist in the Army instead? Apparently, the Navy didn't think I was sea-worthy because a childhood case of rheumatic fever had left me with a slight, but detectable heart murmur. The Army wasn't as selective, otherwise this book would have never been written.

There was, however, a more immediate reason for the timing of my enlistment; it can be found in the storied legend of the French Foreign Legion. I was tempted to do just that but was forced to reconsider upon learning how the French pronounce the word violá (the Italian word for a small violin), and, more to importantly, that the word for "duck" involves five syllables (*canard vers le bas*). The difference may account, in part, for Napoleon's defeat at Waterloo. My theory about this battle is more fully discussed in the opening chapter.

Anyway, the reason I chose to write a humorous account of my time in the Army is much simpler. The experience was, in retrospect, laughable, if not hilarious. While the reader may find this a stretch, they would not do so, had they read one of the great books of the 20th Century, Joseph Heller's *Catch 22*—the acclaimed, truly humorous, account of the real-life experiences of a WWII Army Air Force combat veteran.

While not suggesting that this book belongs on the same library shelf as Heller's book, I'm sure we all can look back and laugh at events in our earlier life that did not seem funny at the time. Similarly, I can now look back at all the pain I endured while standing and marching on fallen arches as being the genesis of this book. However, if you don't see the humor in flat feet being responsible for writing a comedy, then you may not find the events in this book as funny as I did, as I relived three of the most evocative years of my life.

Note: Photos at the end of the book were taken at the time of the depicted events and are un-retouched. Most were taken with the writer's black-and-white Kodak "Brownie" camera, while those taken during basic training were copied from Jostens Military Publications' graduation yearbook—Company N Graduation Date–November 26, 1965.

CHAPTER 1
– Swearing in Ceremony – Whitehall Street,
New York City – September 1965

What did I step into?

Everyone who enters any branch of the US military, from the Coast Guard to the National Guard, shares two common experiences. One of these involves an act of "swearing," which our drill instructors raised to an art form. But before we were permitted to participate in this solemn ritual, we all had to complete an Admissions Application, which required entering a lot of personal information and being fingerprinted for a background check. This was to ensure that no other branch of the government, like the Department of Correction, had a prior claim on your time.

In my case, after completing the application process for entry into the Army, I was sent to a military hospital on Governor's Island off the tip of Manhattan, where I was given an EKG (electrocardiogram). This is what happens when you check off things like having had Rheumatic Fever, as a child. While the Navy had turned me down for this reason, apparently the Army was only marginally concerned with my heart. This makes perfect sense, given R. Lee Ermey's famous quote in *Full Metal Jacket*... "You can give your heart to Jesus, but your ass belongs to the Corps" (the Army in my case).

In retrospect, I wish the doctor had checked my feet instead of my heart, as it later became painfully obvious that I had flat feet, which is the worst affliction a soldier can have, next to myopia. And given the long hours I was forced to stand in line, I developed a personal aversion, if not phobia, to anything resembling one. In fact, I don't recall sitting down for more than brief periods the entire time I was in basic training. This is only logical, given that there weren't many places to sit, unless you count the latrine as one, or a closely related facility called the mess hall. And you often had to stand in line at those facilities, and someone was always waiting to take your seat away, as soon as you sat down.

I did later realize that always being on your feet was of a great benefit, as it resulted in a quasi-form of sleep deprivation, which I believe is the most effective method of preparing a soldier for real combat. That is in comparison to bayoneting dummies or shooting at things that didn't hide, move, or shoot back, at any rate.

There was another interesting thing I discovered about standing all the time. I heard somewhere that the horse and giraffe are the only animals that can sleep standing up. If that's true, I should be in the *Guinness Book of Records,* as I'm living proof that, given enough incentive, humans can do the same. Moreover, given the damage basic training did to my already flat feet, I believe the Army should recognize that the pain and suffering, and resultant damage to the psyche, as a service-related disability. And given the Army's penchant for acronyms, I can offer one to cover that malady "FTA," short for "Foot Travel Aversion." (More about these initials in the next chapter.)

Following my tour of duty, my fear of standing in line calmed when I found an apartment within a block of the MTA's Bronx New York Parkchester train station. Even better, the station ran an express train to within a few blocks of the Manhattan office buildings I'd worked in for ten years in the 1970's. And my aversion to standing for any length of time had another unintended, but positive, consequence: I found a desk job that also required an ability to dictate business letters using the King's English. This, plus the fact that I was able to enjoy my love of reading during the commute on the #6 IRT line, led to a bit of a facility for the written word, which doesn't hurt if you are going to write a book.

Thus, in a world searching for answers, I can recommend that everyone cultivate standing in long lines and experiencing sleep deprivation. Doing so will prepare them for any eventuality, from writing a novel to repelling an invasion. But I'm getting ahead of myself, which is not unusual—I haven't even been sworn in yet.

Following my heart's clean bill of health, as far as the Army was concerned, I was told to report to 39 Whitehall Street in Manhattan, New York at 7 AM on Monday, September 20, 1965 for the formal swearing in ceremony, which is conducted by an Army officer. Before the ceremony began, an NCO (Non-Commissioned Officer, typically a sergeant)—walked us through the process and helped us line up in some semblance of order. We were also shown which hand to raise (the right one) when being sworn in, which marks the first of many occasions in which the Army was to prove that the entire organization was geared to the functionality of those who had to listen carefully when a flight attendant explained how to fasten a seat belt. The Army was gentle about this at first, and if someone accidentally raised their left hand, they were told to raise their "other" right hand.

Now came what was for me the most moving part. An officer entered, and after a few comments about the meaning of the Oath of Allegiance, we were told to raise our right hand and repeat the following:

I, (each of us recited our full name), do solemnly swear that I will support and defend the Constitution of the United States against all enemies, foreign and domestic; that I will bear true faith and allegiance to the same; and that I will obey the orders of the President of the United States and the orders of the Officers appointed over me, according to Regulations and the Uniform Code of Military Justice. So help me God.

(Wait till the ACLU hears about that one!)

We were then told to put our arms down (now that we were officially in the military, we had to get accustomed to taking orders) and that from thereafter, we were to address all officers as "Sir" and all enlisted men by their rank; like Corporal Agar or Sergeant Snorkel, and so on. The only problem with that, at this stage anyway, was I—and a lot of others—had trouble recognizing the difference. Perhaps thinking it's always better to say things like "what a cute girl" when you're not sure of a baby's sex (mothers don't mind if the baby happens to be a boy), we began to say "Yes sir" and "No sir," only to be yelled at for calling a sergeant "Sir," as he would emphatically explain, he "works for a living."

Since I was brainwashed from early on to respond appropriately when yelled at, I immediately realized that sergeants must be the ones in charge, as they had big yellow stripes and yelled all the time, while officers wore little thingamajigs on their collars, or even stars if they were well behaved.

In retrospect, I realized that the Army (I'm sure it's the same for all branches) decided that one of the best ways to get soldiers ready for combat, or to keep them razor sharp after training, was to harass the shit out of them, every time they had a chance. This was also the surest way to weed out the malcontents and unworthy. Aside from having to repeatedly scream responses at the top of our lungs, the first week at the reception center (to which we were bused following the swearing in ceremony) was relaxed compared with what was to follow. I guess all that yelling made the sergeants deaf, which must be the reason they would always shout "I can't hear you," no matter how loud we yelled.

And so it went. But the real story would begin soon. I was about to board a bus to a place totally alien to civilian life. It would be like waking up from a deep sleep and finding myself in a foreign land . . .

CHAPTER 2
– Fort Dix, NJ Reception Center – September 1965

From White Hall Street to halfway round the world

The Reception Center* at Fort Dix, New Jersey, in retrospect could have been more appropriately named the "Deception Center," since it lulled us into a false sense of security from what was to follow. Sort of like the calm before the storm. But before going into all that, I should note that my first "exposure" to Army life enlightened me to the fact that our nation's Founding Fathers never had to stand in line without their clothes on when they wrote that "all men are created equal." Had they done so they might have included an amendment excepting Army Privates. This might have lessened the anxiety of those who were not endowed with the physical assets of others, thereby leaving them to ponder if they were less deserving of citizenship then those who, through an indifferent Mother Nature, were able to proudly display their symbols of American patriotism. However, this display resulted in an ameliorating theory of mine that postulated that those less endowed had more to prove and would therefore make better foxhole buddies than those with more to lose, so to speak. However, asking someone about their endowment could be misread. Happily, I never had to test the theory.

But this postulation might explain why Napoleon Bonaparte tried to conquer all of Europe. Was it perhaps the only way he could impress Empress Josephine? Meaning no disre-

---

* One of many oxymorons I was to encounter in the Army, like "First Priority," "Stand down," and "Military Intelligence."

spect to the French nation, perhaps the artists who painted Napoleon's portraits showing his hand inside his waistcoat did this because they didn't want posterity to know where it was more often situated? Makes one wonder if all the great military leaders throughout history were similarly motivated?

Foregoing further considerations about my theory, except to note that it could be thought of as the first "Peter Principle," I must now outline what I saw, only in retrospect, as the Army's first attempts to cram an amazingly diverse group of physical and philosophical specimens into a single mold, *i.e.,* the "Ultimate Warrior." I bought into the program, as I was out to prove something to myself, my family, friends, God and Country, but most importantly—the opposite sex.

The group that got off the bus with me at the reception center in the mid-nineteen sixties ran the gamut in terms of dress and hairstyle—from those whose Afros could barely fit under a pup tent (later on that) and were sporting clothing in a rainbow of colors, to those who wanted to impress their preparedness with military crew cuts and colorless shirts and pants. The Army's initial answer to this variety was shortly thereafter realized when a team of about ten civilian barbers ran electric shavers, set at zero, over everyone's heads, beards and mustaches—leaving all of us looking like plucked chickens, in what seemed like a matter of seconds. I understand this is no longer the case, as the current all-volunteer Army now gets to keep some of their dos and can't be abused with abandon, either. *Candy asses!*

I was amazed at the amount of hair that piled up on the floor and wondered if the barbers shouldn't be wearing hip-high wading boots, with fly paper draped about them to catch any dislodged critters. No wonder there were "No Smoking" signs posted everywhere. If someone carelessly dropped a match or lit cigarette, the flash fire would have been visible from space.

I later realized the benefit of this clipping operation was two-fold: It not only immediately cut us all down a few notches, but it was very sanitary since it removed the hiding place for any critters that might have hitched a ride with a few of the shaggier types. Boy, the Army sure was smart! Well, not so fast, the next Army exercise was to prove, again in retrospect, that there was still room for improvement in their "Universal Warrior" mold . . .

Not sure what day it was, but the next equalizer occurred when we changed from our civilian montage of dress to one of olive drab. This changed in later years to camouflaged dress. But in 1965, it was olive drab fatigues, hat, coat, socks, etc. Dress shoes and boots were black, and skivvies were white (crew cut shirts and boxer pants). Once thus outfitted, we were forced to relinquish anything that connected us to our former status as a civilian, including most of the contents of our wallets. The only exception was that we were allowed a few personal effects like a comb, or a photo of a girlfriend — which allowed us to maintain a tenuous connection to our former lives. This calls to mind an old joke about the Foreign Legionnaire's habit of carrying a photo of his girlfriend, which, after a long stretch in the desert, was often a camel — the two-hump variety being preferred.

Anyway, this de-civilianization process started with our stripping down to skivvies, so we could be measured, including our hat, neck, waist, inseam, shirt, jacket and shoe size, etc. These statistics allowed for the Army to produce, as if by magic, a seemingly endless supply of clothes that would have humbled every American retailer — that is, up to the advent of Amazon Prime.

Unfortunately, back then the Army didn't issue half sizes, and some things didn't always fit as well as they might. I was 5'-10" and 195 lbs. when I entered the Army, and a 35-1/2" waste and 45-1/2" jacket size, which meant I was issued

36" waist pants and shirts to match. And the ill-fitting clothing I was issued got more ill-fitting by the week. By the time I graduated, I'd lost 2-1/2" off my waist and two full Jacket sizes—which is my earlier point.

Oh, I nearly forgot: As soon as we were finished being outfitted, we had to stencil everything with our last name and serial number. This operation became another of the Army's way of making everything uniform. We quickly got into the habit of addressing each other by our last names, which appeared on our fatigue shirts just above our right pocket once we finished basic training. No more "Osceola, Bobby or Donny" – it was Nordstrom, Merchant, or Rush. This often led to nicknames like Merch and Rusty.

Another way the Army managed to mold the recruits into the universal warrior mold began to materialize during basic training, which was a marvel. While we all ate the same basic food (more about that later) and participated in the same physical activities, guys like me lost 20 pounds, and inches off their waists. 150-pound guys put on 15 or 20 pounds of muscle. As a result, two guys who started out four sizes different in pants and jackets could wear the same size uniforms upon graduation. The waste is that, by the end of basic training, many of us either had trouble squeezing into our uniforms or else walked around wearing baggy clown suits.

Now, if the Army were smarter, it would have withheld its final issuing of clothing until the last week or so of basic training. This would have saved John and Jane Taxpayer from the cost of uniforms that no longer fit, as well as for the ones issued to those who didn't make it through basic training for one reason or another. Not to mention the fact that waiting until the final weeks would have produced much better-looking enlistment poster graduates!

I am compelled to enter other details of Army life that you may find boring, including an explanation and description of things like an enlisted man's rank, pay, dog tags and photo ID. They were part of everyday Army life and I thought they should be entered, accordingly. A civilian enters the Army at its lowest rank, *i.e.*, Private E-1. And until, or if ever, promoted to Private First Class (PFC) E-3, their uniforms were stripeless (like Beetle Bailey). A PFC gets to show off one stripe, a Corporal, two, a buck Sergeant three, and so on. If I recall, the pay in 1965 for a private E-1 was $45.00 per month. Not much to live on, until you consider that the food, housing, and clothing were free, and a bottle of beer cost twenty-five cents. Upon graduating from basic training, we were all promoted to private E-2. Still no stripes, but a bit more to put in our empty wallets. I didn't make PFC E-3 until May of the following year, but quickly rose in rank thereafter to Sergeant E-5. In retrospect, I know it took a great deal of work on my part, which I'll go into later, but I also know that there was more than a bit of luck involved in terms of timing, since a lot of unconnected moving parts had to come one after another in quick succession.

Another symbol of the Army's uniformity was "dog tags," which we got accustomed to wearing 24-7 (even in the shower). While one might think the name has something to do with barking sergeants or aching feet, it came from the fact that the ones worn during the "Great War" (as it was then called) and WWII were round, and resembled the tags that dogs wore. The shape was changed during the Korean Conflict to the rectangular tags with rounded edges that the military now employs. They were made of stainless steel and were hung from a one size fits all BB style chain around our necks. We were issued two in case of accidental death* or

---

* I use the term "accidental death" as we were told that anyone getting themselves killed without permission was tantamount to being permanently AWOL (Absent Without Leave), which was a serious military breach, warranting severe punishment.

dismemberment, one being kept with the body and the other kept with the soldiers' medical records. Dog tags are embossed with the name, serial number, blood type and religious preference of the wearer, with the last name of the individual being listed first.

This reminds me of another odd thing about the Army; the names of things were always listed in reverse order. For example, "Black Dress Shoes" were listed as "Shoes, Dress, Black, and the small foldable shovel issued to us was designated as "Tool, Entrenching." This often led to problems when the need arose to order spare parts. For example, if you needed to order a replacement for a truck's drive shaft, it would be found under the heading "Vehicle, M151 (the technical name for a Jeep), Drive Shaft. It's a bit like trying to find the correct spelling of a word you don't know how to spell.

Another item we all were required to have on our person at all times was a laminated photo ID card. Mine contained a picture of a bald and scary looking recruit and looked like it was taken with an outdated black and white camera whose resolution was such that it would have stumped today's most advanced facial recognition software.

My ID card also contained my birth date, height and weight, the color of my hair and eyes, as well as the date of service entry, service number (Mine was RAXXXX2652), blood type, and religious preference. Incidentally, the "RA" initials preceding my serial number, stood for "Regular Army" which distinguished those who enlisted in the Army from those whose number had come up in the draft. The draftee's serial number contained the prefix "US," as in United States.

One creative thing about GI's was, and I'm sure still is, an ability to express things like "RA" and "US" in more explicit terms, usually involving four letter words. Thus, the initials "RA" translated as "Regular Asshole." And if a civilian were to inquire, these terms of endearment would be less offensive, such as the initials "US" "Unfortunate Soul," in lieu of "Unlucky Slob." Readers are invited to substitute their own words when considering the Army's penchant for using initials and acronyms for every conceivable matter. This turns out to be a great segue to my final comments on the events that transpired during my sojourn at the Reception Center.

Before moving on, I would be remiss if I didn't relate one more detail from my days at the reception center. I recall the event as if it were yesterday. I was walking to one of the Army's more aptly named venues, *i.e.*, the "mess hall" with a group of GIs' ("General Issue"—WWII term). As I was about to enter my first "mess," I saw that someone had written upon the mess hall's entrance wall. There I beheld "FTA" in large painted letters, with the words, "Fun-Travel-Adventure" scribbled below it. I was to later learn the letters also could be taken to mean "Finest Training Available." I would remind you here of the "old army axiom" that prefaced this book and leave any alternate interpretations of the initials to the creativity of the reader.

But back to our story: It was time to move on. I was beginning to think that Army life wasn't too difficult to take, but I was in for a rude awakening . . .

CHAPTER 3

– Fort Dix, NJ Basic Training Center – Home of the "Ultimate Warrior" – Company N - 3rd Training Brigade October-November 1965

The "Ultimate Warrior"

The bus ride from the reception center to the WWII barracks we were to call home for the next eight weeks was relatively short, but it quickly became apparent we were no longer in Kansas. While we expected things to be a bit more formal than the semi-relaxed atmosphere of the reception center, nothing prepared us for the stunning experience we were about to encounter. If they had only made movies like *Full Metal Jacket* back then, we might have been better prepared for our drill instructors near flawless impersonations of R. Lee Ermey. Unfortunately, we were consigned to play the role of hapless stooges without the benefit of any rehearsal, and, in retrospect, we were perfect on the first take. Having total recall about such traumatic events, I have replayed the scene more than once.

A short, but stunningly aggressive Drill Instructor, SFC Maylon C. Breen, boarded the bus which housed about 60 of us, together with our oversized duffle bags, and began to scream and curse at us with such force that we were all stunned into momentary paralysis. Somehow, amid the screams and curses, we were able to deduce the fact that we had one minute to get off the bus and form-up (whatever the hell that meant) and that anyone remaining on the bus after the one minute was up would wish their mothers had never met their fathers (to borrow a line from the movie *Jaws*– which seems appropriate for the occasion).

As the group began to rush off the bus, Sgt. Breen began intoning the seconds as they elapsed. Being quick at arithmetic and spatial concepts, I began to wish that a few more of the recruits' moms and dads had postponed their engagement a bit, as the bus wasn't half empty when "30 seconds" was shouted, as I waited my turn at the back of the bus. I doubt if you will believe this, but considering that mortals can exhibit super human strength when their life depends on it, you will cut me some slack when I tell you that I ran from the back of the bus to the front of the bus during the final countdown with my right arm fully extended, shoulder height, over the seat backs. Big deal you say, until I tell you that my 85-pound duffle bag was clutched in my right hand, and it never once got caught in the seats. I swear this is true. And if you can picture this you will be able to connect to the moment.

In later life, while trying to repeat this feat of strength by using my right arm as a cannon, I paid the price via rotator cuff surgery. Speaking of cannons, and as a way of paying tribute to the Ringling Bros. and Barnum & Bailey Circus (which folded its tent in 2017), I'm reminded of the sad tale of the circus's human cannonball, the "Great Zucchini" who died tragically after he went on a crash diet and overshot the catch net. His epitaph read:

There will never be another man of his caliber.

While it may seem odd to find anecdotes such as this in a work of non-fiction, I couldn't resist the temptation. Hopefully, you will not take exception on this entry, as there will be many more of the same— and you don't want to waste your ammo until you find a more deserving target.

Being one of the last off the bus had its benefits though, as the welcoming committee of Drill Instructors was busy terrorizing those who exited earlier. Some unlucky SOB's were running around the scrum with their duffle bags over their heads, for some infraction or other. I was to see a similar act repeated, after we were issued our rifles, which were told to refer to as a "rifle," an "M-14," a "weapon," or a "piece," but never, ever, a "gun!" Anyone familiar with a similar scene in *Full Metal Jacket* may recall the exact words used, but in our case the guilty party had to run around the barracks holding his rifle above his head with one hand, while clutching his crotch with the other one, shouting repeatedly "This is my rifle! This is my gun! This is for fighting! . . ."

Another thing I recall about that first day is it was hot, and we were sweating like pigs.* Somehow, out of all the initial chaos, our platoon was arranged into four squads, by height as I recall, and assigned bunks and footlockers. Our sleeping accommodations consisted of two white folded sheets, pillowcase, two brown wool blankets, and a striped pillow stacked on a striped mattress folded on the double-tiered, metal- framed bunk bed. The bunks had springs clipped into holes around the edges of the bed frame and connected to a supporting wire lattice.

I took the top bunk as I didn't want someone sleeping over me. We were allowed time to make our bunks and put away our clothing and gear, with orders to fall out for evening mess at 16:30 hours, which is 4:30 PM to civilians. For those who are interested, an easy way to convert military time to civilian time is to add one hundred to the AM hours and twelve hundred to the PM hours. Thus 1 AM becomes 01:00 (pronounced "O-one hundred hours"), etc. and 1 PM becomes 13:00 hours (pronounced "thirteen hundred hours"). 2 PM becomes 1400 and so on.

---

* For those who, like me, wonder where an idiomatic expression like this came from, it appears to relate to the shape of smelted raw ingots of iron which resembled a pig, *ergo* pig iron.

The Army had a simpler solution, you could buy a 24 hour, waterproof and shockproof wristwatch in the PX (Post Exchange) for about ten dollars. While the term Post Exchange was originally akin to a trading post, they no longer accept hides in trade; luckily for us.

Basic training also taught us that, except for being told how to tie our shoes, everything had to be done the "Army" way. We were shown how to make our bunks so tight that a quarter would bounce off them. Boy was I lucky to have taken the top bunk; the poor schmucks who happily grabbed the lower bunks now had to lie on the floor under their bunks to tighten them up by pulling in on the blankets. Speaking of which reminds me of another reason I suffered from sleep deprivation, as well a good reason to re-invoke the memories of the Ringling Bros. and Barnum & Bailey Circus.

But before getting to that I should explain that our training regimen started with reveille blaring at 5:30 AM, and didn't end until we had finished the evening spit-shinning our shoes and cleaning our weapons, and were all dead tired by the time Taps echoed its melancholy call across the camp, marking the 10 PM lights-out hour. While some recruits claimed that the sudden loss of appetite for the fairer sex was because the Army put sodium nitrate (saltpeter) in our food, I doubted that was necessary since my own get up and go had gotten up and gone after the first couple of days.

One night, after pulling KP (kitchen police) duty, which typically involved a 4:30 AM wake-up call, I accidentally discovered another significant military asset one can possess, aside from having good arches and eyesight: a large bladder. Think about it. How many soldier's advancement, and maybe even safety, may have been compromised by having to take a leak at an inopportune time.

And while civilian pants have zippers to speed the process, our fatigues had button-up flies. I can only imagine how time consuming it was to relieve oneself with the flap buttoned trousers once worn by soldiers, or worse still, the fly-less pantaloons of yore. Maybe even some important battles were lost because of it—makes you wonder about Napoleon's defeat at a place named "Waterloo."

Anyhow, after returning from KP one night I as too tired to relieve myself before I hit the sack (a Navy term for the hammocks sailors once slept on) and quickly fell asleep. Unfortunately, nature reminded me of my miscalculation in the middle of the night, so I had to get up and correct the oversight. As I corrected accounts, I let go with a loud sigh while thinking that there was no better feeling (well almost). The "aaaaah" moment however was short-lived as, once I got back into my bunk and adjusted my pillow, I suddenly realized that the room was alive with every kind of sound an exhausted group of 60 men can expel when sleeping. Those who weren't snoring seemed to let out an involuntary sigh or gasp every few seconds.

I wrapped my pillow around my ears to try to muffle the sounds, but it was impossible. What could I do to quiet this cacophony long enough to get to sleep? Then it hit me: *Viola!*— I had the solution. As I lay there in the dark, I let out a primordial scream that could be heard a mile away. Everyone woke up and began yelling what the hell happened. Someone turned on the lights to see if anyone had been killed and a few men jumped out of their bunks and ran outside as if being told to fall out.

As the panic began to subside, the lights were turned out and everyone got back into bunks and mumbled back to sleep. The trick now was to get to sleep before the three-ringed circus returned. I soon fell into a blissful sleep and enjoyed all the banter the next morning; it seemed no one knew what had happened, or what had caused whatever had happened, or even where the whatever happened had happened.

I offered that someone, or something, must have had a bad dream. Since it was thought that bears inhabited the Pine Barrens where we trained, the "something" was plausible.

A few more things about the barracks and sleeping with 60 guys for eight weeks: Once we got to know each other (the term "misery loves company" comes to mind), we developed friendships—and with that we began to play practical jokes on each other. One of the favorites was the old "short sheet" trick. When short-sheeted, some unsuspecting Joe would try to get under the sheets of his bunk, only to discover that someone had folded the sheets over themselves, halfway up. So, when the dead tired target tried to get into his bunk, he couldn't slide his feet very far down. This resulted in a chorus of curses while the bedding was torn down, which was naturally greeted by a good deal of laughter.

Less-liked or slacker types who slept on a bottom bunk might receive a more heinous treatment. By the way, if a reader ever needs help relieving a kidney or two, this treatment will work well, except I would not recommend it be tried in bed. Anyway, after the victim had fallen asleep, one of his hands was slowly placed in a bucket of warm water. Almost 100% guaranteed, if he didn't wake up from feeling the warm liquid in the bucket, he'd wake up from the warm liquid that accumulated in his bedding.

Another training custom we learned was that we were always expected to be on time, which in Army parlance meant 15 minutes early. This gave way to another tried and true Army euphemism, "Hurry up and wait"—and arriving early always insured you would be doing both.

Now seems like an appropriate time to discuss the Army's version of *The Gourmet Cook*, namely *The Venerable Mess Hall Cooks*. There is a saying that an Army moves on its stomach, and looking at the size of some of those who chose to be cooks, it's easy to see why. One reminded me of a mess hall sergeant named "Cookie." For those who don't know who he is, his image can be found among the myriad copies of Mort Walker's *Beetle Bailey* newspaper cartoons. I could illustrate a few of my favorites, but that would be going too far out of bounds, even for me.

I was later to learn just how most Army cooks got to be Army cooks, and, I can assure you, it wasn't because they had gone to the Culinary Institute. It seemed that, while enlistees could choose either their job, or as it is known, "Military Occupational Skill (MOS)" or "duty station," it appeared that those who were drafted were assigned an MOS that involved anything *but* whatever occupation they practiced as a civilian. For example, someone who rebuilt truck motors for a living was sure to be made a cook and a hash slinger from Sloppy Joe's All-Night Diner was destined to find himself replacing a truck's rear axle. To the Army, this made perfect sense; as I alluded to earlier, the Army's strategy to sharpen a soldier's fighting ability to a keen edge was to make him as uncomfortable and angry as possible so he would have something to look forward to if they ever got into a shooting war. This truism about how the Army selected its cooks may have given rise to an old joke about a US Army cook becoming one of the most highly decorated soldiers in WWII—by the German High Command.

Another thing I learned during the first few weeks of basic training reinforced the credo that the Army moves on its belly. Aside from that being the best position to be in when the bullets start flying, the Army, to foster discipline, wanted all its recruits to pull KP duty. But peeling 100 lbs. of potatoes resulted in a different outcome than intended, i.e.,,, stupid potato jokes like, "What's the difference between mashed potatoes and pea soup? The answer: "Anyone can mash potatoes." Aside from helping to prepare meals, KP included cleaning up after a very large group of sloppy eaters three times a day, as well as scrubbing floors and scouring the largest pots and pans I'd ever seen.

Incidentally, the term "police" (as in KP) applied to other activities, such as picking up carelessly discarded cigarette butts—known as "policing the area." And if someone were caught carelessly discarding one, they might end up having to give it a Christian burial. The only benefit I can recall from pulling KP was that I quickly crossed off the restaurant business and cleaning service industry from my list of future employment opportunities. Aside from the endless day when assigned to KP, or night when on guard duty (in our case it was barracks fire watch) the time span from the start of basic training to graduation whizzed by quickly.

While on the subject KP (and guard duty), in addition to the Army tradition of never being wrong (a truism I alluded to in the opening pages of this book), another Army axiom was "never volunteer for anything." As it turned out, this wasn't necessary. As with KP and guard duty, the Army saved us from the stress of "should-I- volunteer-or-shouldn't-I" decisions, as it was perfectly willing to volunteer any of us whenever the need arose.

This reminds me of one of the many jokes I heard in the Army, most of which couldn't be repeated—not because they were too bawdy, but because they were so bad as to cause the more erudite reader to skip a meal. The following offering is about a private who was "volunteered" for a top-secret training mission involving the delivery of a coded message to a heavily fortified base in an advance combat area (meaning surrounded by the enemy).

The plan required a private for this mission because the Army wanted to insure the operation was so simple that it could be successfully completed by any soldier, including the guy who was still listening to the flight attendant's instruction on how to fasten a seat belt. Anyhow, the mission was meticulously planned so the volunteer wouldn't have to decide anything more taxing than which leg to put into his pants first. And if successful, the planning would be shown to be completely foolproof. The mission would require total secrecy and silence and, above all, precise timing. The operation was to start with the private boarding a plane at exactly 0200 hours. The plane would fly for two hours, at an altitude of exactly 15,000 feet, to the drop zone marked on a map. The private was to then parachute out at exactly 0400 hours and would be met by a jeep which would whisk him to the command post.

Unfortunately, things went wrong from the get-go. The plane scheduled for the operation was out of service, so a small single engine trainer had to be substituted at the last minute. When the private was told this, he murmured to himself, "&%$# Army." When it wasn't cleared to take off until 0300, he again murmured "&%$# Army" a few more times. Since the plane was slower than the originally intended one, the private was told it would now take three hours to reach the drop zone, prompting a few more under-the-breath mutterings of "&%$# Army." Then he was told that the plane couldn't fly at 15,000 feet and he'd have to jump at 5,000 feet, bringing another teeth-gritted "&%$# Army."

Finally, as dawn was approaching, he was told to jump. Murmuring more curses, he jumped and began counting. When he reached ten, he pulled the rip cord on his main chute, which failed to open – more mumbled "&%$# Army." He then pulled the cord on his reserve chute cord. When it failed to immediately deploy, he began to curse the Army out load. He continued to yank on the cord until he realized it wasn't going to open in time, resulting in his last words, now shouted at the top of his lungs, "&%$# Army," "I'll bet the fucking jeep ain't there either!"

During my eight weeks of basic training starting in September of 1965 (It's now ten weeks, perhaps to better prepare the modern trainees for missions like the one recorded above), we marched or double-timed everywhere—except I recall being trucked to the rifle range. The good thing was that by now even the guy who needed instructions on fastening a safety belt had learned that we only have one left foot and one right foot—so the drill instructor didn't have to keep repeating that he was referring to our other left foot. This was very important when marching in a close formation or slinging a rifle around while performing the Manual of Arms.

To help us keep in step, we often sang cadence songs like the vulgar ones immortalized by the late R. Lee Ermey in the film *Full Metal Jacket*—"I don't know, but I've been told . . . Eskimo (pie) is mighty cold." YouTube has the complete repertoire on-line, if one is interested. This was all part of our daily physical training (PT) which included jogging "double time" from one training venue to another, guaranteeing most of us would pass-out if allowed to sit down. But unless one was part horse (or mule which is the Army's mascot), sleep deprivation turned out to be a positive—at least for me.

Of the many things we had to memorize during basic training, (like our serial number—I still remember mine) the one I found most difficult was the ten (now eleven) General Orders. This was a list that described a soldier's duties while standing (ouch!) guard. As with all things, the Army sought a means to simplify the task of learning these orders and came upon a foolproof method. It was related to the axiom that necessity is the mother of invention, or in this case, retention.

The necessity in this case was the desire to have PX and movie privileges. Also, after the first month, families—or more importantly girlfriends—would be allowed weekend visits. All of which was dependent upon us learning the General Orders. The incentive was so strong that I still recall a few, even after 54 years, including, "To quit my post only when properly relieved." I have my flat feet to thank for the amazing retention of this one out of all the others.

We were also taught everything there was to know about an M-14 rifle, which was our "best friend," including how to disassemble and re-assemble it in the dark. We were told that using a flashlight in the event your rifle jammed would not be a good idea. Once issued to us, we carried it virtually everywhere and learned the Manual of Arms (right shoulder arms, left shoulder arms, etc.) Finally, we were shown how to load, aim, and (hopefully) fire it with some degree of accuracy. Some guys were a lot better at this than others and earned an "Expert" rating. I was rated as a sharpshooter, which will be explained below. We also received a few days' training in the use of a bayonet and hand-to-hand combat. The main thing I took away from these exercises is the importance of keeping my rifle clean and becoming a good shot.

Another exercise in military discipline came in the form of daily inspections of the cleanliness of our rifles, the spit-and-polish of our shoes, boots, and the like, as well as personal hygiene. Clean shaves and haircuts were a must. The toughest inspections occurred every Saturday morning, and included our uniforms, bunks, foot and wall lockers, the barracks, and latrines. The floors were the most difficult to clean, as they were covered with a reddish Masonite—and while easily cleaned and polished to a high luster, readily showed footprints. For this reason, the floors were the last thing we tackled, as foot traffic was not possible once they were cleaned and waxed and buffed.

On the morning of the inspection we'd buff the floor one last time and scramble around in stocking feet with towels to wipe the floors clear up to where we stood for inspection. Friday night cleaning (or "GI-ing" as we called it) was accompanied by a radio blaring out the latest rock-n-roll hits of the day. The Rolling Stones *I Can't Get No Satisfaction* (the Stones sure knew how to rub it in), and *Get Off of My Cloud* (*Two's a Crowd?*—not likely), *1-2-3* by Len Barry (he forgot to say "hep"), and *Wooly Bully*. *Matty Told Hatty?*—no one knows to this day what the hell Sam and Shams were talking about. The great thing is we almost forgot that we were cleaning as we sang and danced. That's why, to this day, cleaning the barracks is called a "GI Party."

After the hours of cleaning on Fridays, we could relax and goof off as only GI's know how. And there was always a lot of competition. Who could spin into a defensive *karate* stance the fastest when tapped on the shoulder, who could do the most push-ups while being tickled, and so on. I let it be known that I was the fastest runner in the barracks. Since the guys knew I ran virtually every night, no one would challenge me, except a black friend, one Friday evening.

The entire platoon watched the race. They cleared the center of the barracks for us. Pvt. Mavis and I went to the far end and took off on the word "Go." We were neck-and-neck for almost the entire length of the barracks, but he wisely backed off a bit as we passed the last bunks. Wanting to best him, I continued all out, raising my arms to stop myself as I hit the wall. Unfortunately, I hadn't counted on the age of the barracks or the thinness of the wall board, as my hands went right through it, leaving two holes and a mess on the floor!

After the laughter died out, I was declared the winner by a nose, which had impacted the wall when my hands failed to do their job. We were quickly able to clean up the mess on the floor, but there was no way to patch the holes in the walls, which were sure to be noticed the next morning when the barracks were inspected. Damage to an Army facility could mean some heavy punishment all around, and the failure to pass an inspection meant confinement to the barracks for sure. There was just no way around it.

The next morning, however, we passed the inspection, as

the holes were nowhere to be seen—proving that desperation can also be the mother of invention. Long gone by now, but if one had a time-machine they would be able to learn how this feat of magic was accomplished. All they would have to do was remove the two Army posters used to cover the holes. Reminds you of a scene from *Shawshank Redemption*, now that I mention it, doesn't it?

This topic reminds me of another interesting event related to my passion for running (long since retired, along with worn out knees). When I was a teenager, I played sand-lot football, and our coach's conditioning program involved practicing in a sand covered lot in the Bronx's Throgs Neck, just outside a summer community known as Edgewater Park. This was akin to a baseball player swinging a weighted bat in the on-deck circle, times ten. Running in sand was like, well, running in sand. The great thing about this, aside from being easy on my feet, is once I hit solid ground it felt like gravity had been temporarily suspended.

Anyway, I saw the sand covered Pine Barrens that surrounded Ft. Dix as the perfect place to build up my endurance and speed and took advantage of it every chance I got. This is also one of the reasons I dropped 20 pounds during basic training and came in second in the mile run we had to complete in less than ten minutes, to graduate basic training. The guy who beat me was a high school miler.

Anyhow, one evening as I was jogging, I neared a small clearing not far from my barracks where three trails came together. I was glad to be nearing the end of my run, as it was getting dark and only the whiteness of the sand paths between the shrub pine and bushes kept me on course. As I entered the clearing I was startled to see a bear sitting at the juncture of two trails.

Never slacking up, I took off running towards the barracks as if my life depended on it, as I thought it did. I was too afraid to even take a backward glance as I recalled Satchel Paige's maxim "never look back as someone might be gaining on you" and, although he may not have had a bear in mind, it was good enough for me.

When I hit the pavement, I took off like a bullet and didn't stop running until I'd reached the barracks. As I cleared the platform at the front door and was reaching for the doorknob, I chanced a micro-second look behind me. With a sigh of relief, I realized that not only had I obviously outrun the bear, but had done it without soiling my pants. For me this added new meaning to the expression "scared shitless"—a phrase coined by someone caught in an outhouse without a Sears catalog during a hurricane.

The next morning, as my fellow Ultimate-Warriors-in-training were standing in line at the mess hall, I snuck off to see if the bear had chased me, and having watched Frank Buck's *Bring'em Back Alive* on early TV shows, I was sure I could tell the difference between bear tracks and my own. Unfortunately, I must have missed the show where Frank tracked a runaway camel in the Sahara, as I could not tell the bears tracks from my own, as the only evidence I found was amorphous depressions in the sand.

Since the wind was in my face and walking in sand doesn't make any noise, I chanced a very careful walk back to the point in the trail where I'd seen the bear the evening before.

While I'm a bit embarrassed to admit it, they say confession is good for the soul (at least that's what the nuns at Our Lady of Grace told me). So I'm conscience-bound to confess that, instead of finding some evidence of the scariest bear I had ever seen, all I found was a small shrub, right where the bear was supposed to be.

Since I'd never heard of a bear planting a shrub, I had to presume that the most likely scenario was that I'd mistaken that bush for a bear. In my defense, it was dark the night before and a breeze had caused the shrub, which was about the size of a bear, to move. Being philosophical about it, I'm sure even Grizzly Adams could have made the same mistake since, contrary to popular belief, old Grizzly was also afraid of stumbling upon one, unannounced. Who in their right mind—or left one for that matter—wouldn't be?

I must take another sidebar here, while on the subject of bears, as this is an opportunity too good to pass up. If memory serves, in 1999 one of the Chicago Bears players, in eulogizing the great Walter Payton* told a story of how "Sweetness" loved the outdoors. And that once when camping out with Payton, the offensive lineman woke up to find Walter putting on his sneakers. He asked Payton why he was doing this in the middle of the night and Walter answered that he heard a bear moving around outside the tent and was "getting the hell out of there."

The player told Walter: that was stupid, as no one could outrun a bear. Walter answered, "probably not, but I can outrun *your* ass." I never told my wife that story, even though she often took our kids camping at Lake Welch (which is only about 10 miles from Bear Mountain, NY) as I didn't want to scare her. Instead, and in tribute to Walter's memory, I always insisted that she take her mother along.

While I'm side-barring about bears, I might as well get this one off my chest as well, as I will be telling you about an unforgettable mid-Westerner I was fortunate enough to have in my outfit. Donald Rush, "Rusty" to his friends, had a way of saying things that kind of stayed with you. Being born in the

---

* Walter Payton was one of the most prolific running backs in NFL history and was inducted into the Hall of Fame in 1993. Mike Ditka, a teammate and Hall of Fame player and NFL coach, described Payton as "The greatest football player he had ever seen – but even greater as a human being."

Bronx, I used expressions like "you bet your ass," when swearing that Sally's tits were as big as melons. Being from a rural area, Rusty would say, in a similar situation, albeit regarding the size of Hilda's Glockenspiel's, "Does a bear shit in the woods?"

I better end these side bars and get back to basic training if I hope to graduate with the rest of the Ultimate Warriors. In order to catch up with the group, I'm going to fast track the rest of the basic training using key words and pithy (I hope) explanations, where appropriate:

Shot Records

When I first saw these words in our upcoming list of activities, I assumed we'd get our first taste of firing our weapons. When we were marched off to a building, I held out hope that it was going to be like a carnival stand where you're given a rifle that emits a beam that knocks down ducks, but that was short lived when we were told to take off our shirts and tie them around our waists.

I quickly learned that the only rifles involved were the guns in the hands of the Army's equivalent of Navy Corpsmen and the rounds that were being used consisted of vaccines for every known malady to man, that we could be immunized against. The shots were administered in alternating shoulders as we "ran the gamut."

Afterward, I was glad that the next few days would not require us to do any heavy lifting, thus further lessening the need for the Army to add saltpeter to our food (small joke).

Guard Duty

In addition to pulling KP once a week we also had guard duty, actually a fire watch. And, as alluded to earlier, we were required to learn the twelve "General Orders"—or be confined to the barracks until we did. And the one about not quitting your post until properly "relieved," provided another opportunity to enhance the capacity of our bladders. Boy, the Army sure thought of everything!

Chain of Command

The Army followed a strict code that required everyone to report to, or obey the orders of, the next higher authority of a unit, who would report to his higher authority and so on, up the line, right up the highest higher authority. I guess that's one of the reasons ole "Give 'em Hell, Harry" (President Truman)* had a sign on his desk that read "The Buck Stops Here." Our top kick (head sergeant) had a much simpler explanation, "Shit flows downhill."

Formation and Marching Commands

These are verbal commands designed to keep raw recruits from stepping on each other's feet. This also kept them from stepping on the heel of the soldier in front of you while marching or jogging. The problem was, as I saw it, being in tight formations allowed an enemy soldier with myopia to be a crack shot. The commands were always given with slurred and elongated first syllables, with the second part of the command consisting of shouted grunts generally emphasizing the letter H, as in "Hut." Maybe that's why foot soldiers are called "grunts." Typical drill instructor commands were:

"Ah-Tennnn—*Hut!*" (Attention)
"Ah-bouououut—*Hace!*"
"Riiiight—*Hace!*"   Fououou-ward – *Harch!*

---

* When asked about this, President Truman remarked, "I just tell them the truth; they *think* it's hell."

I came up with a theory of where these ridiculous sounding commands originated after reading about Prussian General Friedrich von Steuben's contribution to our Revolutionary war effort. Von Steuben was credited for instilling military discipline while training Washington's rag-tag volunteer army in close order drill, at Valley Forge. What was even more remarkable was that von Steuben couldn't speak a word of English.

Manual of Arms

This is a series of movements we learned for handling a rifle in formation or while marching. This was essential to prevent soldiers from being injured by friendly fire or, in this case, being hit in the head with a rifle butt, and vice-versa. Commands included words like "Right Shoulderrrr – Arms," "Preee-sent – Arms," etc. Since these commands are closer to normal English, my guess is old General von Steuben must have improved his English to insure the militia understood what they were doing, once they had the more than six feet long muskets and bayonets in their hands.

"Spit-Shined" Shoes

The Army took great pride in requiring its recruits to shine their shoes and boots to such a high luster that the wearer could see his face in them. This has many advantages including looking around corners or up a girl's dress without making it too obvious. I'm not sure that's what the Army Brass had that in mind, but I wouldn't put it past them either.

Incidentally, for those who might want to use a pair of shoes as a mirror in a pinch, the method only requires a little shoe polish, some spit (tap water works as well) and lots of elbow grease. The trick is to wrap a soft piece of cotton cloth around one or two fingertips and then repeatedly dip them lightly into the water and a dab of shoe polish (the same color as the shoes works best) and rub the mixture in a circular motion into the leather. If you repeat this for a few hours, you will be amazed at the result. You can, of course buy or rent a pair of shoes like this and save your fingers tips from becoming the color of your shoes until your body replaces the skin.

Rifle Training

Before we were permitted to fire our M-14's we had to learn to take them apart and reassemble them in a few minutes—blindfolded. As alluded to above, I immediately realized the sagacity of this, as the alternative, *i.e.*, using a flashlight to clear a jammed rifle at the wrong time might also result in becoming permanently AWOL, the result of which was discussed earlier.

After a week of training in the finer points of using this 8-pound weapon, we were taken to a firing range and issued live ammunition—initially, one 7.62mm round at a time. The first thing we learned was how to "zero in" the rifle, which involved adjusting the rear slotted sight a bit left or right and up and down, so the round landed where it was aimed. This was done by firing at a close target and adjusting the rifle's sights, until you could repeatedly hit the target in the same location. Unfortunately, this also deprived us an excuse for missing the target at further distances, as it was unlikely that the enemy would stand a short distance away while we carefully took aim at them.

The "aim" of this next exercise was to have three rounds fired consecutively hit the target in a grouping. If the three rounds left holes that touched each other, it was called a "Ballantine," after the name of the one-time New York brewer, whose label contained three overlapping rings. For old Yankee fans like me, you may recall sportscaster Mel Allen's unmistakable Southern twangy voice call, "It's a Ballantine Blast" as he announced another Bronx Bomber home run.

Once we mastered hitting a target with a repeatable result, we moved on to targets that were further distant, until we were firing at targets that were hundreds of yards away (a football field is 100 yards long). At these distances, the front sight of the rifle completely covered the target, which was the size of a man. It took a very steady hand and keen eye to hit a target that far away. Amazingly, our instructor was able to repeatedly hit targets at 400 yards distance with seeming ease. He was so good, we joked that his picture was on *Not* Wanted posters in carnivals in all 50 states and most of the commonwealth nations, too.

In order to graduate basic training, we had to qualify by hitting a target that was 200 yards away. The three passing grades were "Expert" (the shooter hit the target 90% of the time), followed by Sharpshooter, which is what I was classified, having hit the target 80% of the time, followed by Marksman, at 65%. (Hopefully, members of this group opted for the Artillery or were sent to the Army's version of the Culinary Institute.)

Training Films

The Army was great on using training films to drive home the dangers that lurked outside getting shot or shelled in combat. The good news was we didn't have to worry about getting shelled, as we were told that if we were within a shell's kill radius, we wouldn't know about it, anyway.

One of the films warned of the dangers of frost bite. We were treated to actual footage of a man's frost bitten and blackened toes being removed with pliers, with gook oozing out. This was done to remind us what can happen if we didn't protect our nose, feet and/or hands from freezing. A similar result came from trench foot, which occurred if the feet were to stay wet, for a lengthy period.

Another film showed mutilated and dismembered bodies

which resulted from car accidents, usually the result of drinking and/or drugs, and even speeding. I remember the film about the dangers of unprotected sex since it reminded me of an old joke about a GI who came down with some unknown venereal disease. When the GI finally found a specialist, who knew about the affliction, he asked in a panic if his blackened private had to be amputated. The doctor told him, "no, that won't be necessary - it will fall off by itself."

Hand to Hand Combat and Bayonet Training

As alluded to above, after stabbing dummies and trying to look like the second coming of Bruce Lee, I decided the more effective and safer option to close-in combat was to improve my aim at the rifle range, and thus avoid it as long as possible. Besides, since I was destined to join the Artillery, I wasn't concerned about coming face to face with the enemy. Particularly since the Artillery isn't allowed to be on the front line, unless the front line was moved without permission, and we know that could have serious disciplinary consequences.

Gas Mask Training

We were taught how to don the clumsy mask quickly and were shown how to give ourselves Atropine shots to counter chemical or nerve agent attacks. While stabbing yourself with a needle doesn't come easy to most, we were assured that given the alternative, we'd do Dr. Kildare proud. To ensure that we wouldn't panic if hit by a sudden attack, we were made to enter a tear gas filled house, remove our mask, and traverse an obstacle course before exiting. This was not an experiment I would recommend you try at home. When we got clear of the building, we were told to flush our face and eyes with water, which helped alleviate the burning a bit.

C-Rations ("C" as in Combat)
—The Army's Answer to Meals in a Box

The Drill Instructor's discussion about the contents of a typical box of C-Rations is one that stayed with me. The contents included a can of bread or fruit cake, a can of meat of some type, a small folding can opener, a pack of gum, a pack of four cigarettes, a book of matches and, the indispensable pack of toilet paper. Unfortunately, the pack only contained one approximate 4"x4" double sheet.

As we pondered how to make do with such a small piece of toilet paper our Drill Instructor came to the rescue, by demonstrating its proper use. He did this by folding the sheet in half and then half again to form a small square. He then tore off a small section from inside corner and told us not to discard it. Instead he placed it in an unbuttoned shirt pocket, as if performing a magic trick. Then putting his index finger through the hole that remained, he reached between his legs and made a sweeping motion as if wiping himself. He then took his free hand and squeezed it around the base of his index finger and began pushing the toilet paper up that finger so to capture the make-believe poop in the sheet. When he reached the top of his index finger, he folded over the ends and advised it was to be properly discarded, along with the main ingredient.

He then reminded us of the small scrap of paper he'd placed in his pocket and holding it aloft said, "use this to clean the shit from under your fingernail."

Weekend Passes

After the first month we were eligible to receive a weekend pass, which allowed us to go off base, assuming we had passed the usual Saturday morning's inspection, and knew our General Orders, of course. We were told to be back before Sunday's bed check. Those of us who didn't have weekend duty and had kept up their training grades could go home for a full day, if they lived within driving distance. A few never returned but, in retrospect, it was good for the Army.

Graduation Day, November 26, 1965

After eight weeks we all felt great to have the training finally come to an end. In the last two weeks prior, our drill instructors had started to lighten up and began talking about their experiences in the Army, and the duty stations where they had served. While we heard stories about Germany and Korea, none of our non-coms had served in the one area which held the most interest for us, Viet Nam ("Nam" to those who served there). Later I was to hear stories from those I knew who served a tour there, but mostly after I was discharged. One supply room sergeant I knew in Germany had done a tour in Nam but had been stationed in a rear area which didn't see any action. He liked the relaxed discipline and hazardous duty pay so much that he said he was looking forward to returning. A rare exception, I'm sure.

Our eight weeks culminated with a multiple unit "Pass in Review" parade, which followed the Commanding General's speech about the meaning of the event. The only thing I remember, other than how much my feet hurt, was looking for the face of my girlfriend among all the family members who were waving as we passed in review. After the ceremony, we were given our orders and leave papers. If I recall, those destined to serve in Viet Nam were sent to camp Lejeune, SC for jungle training.

I was not to be one of them . . .

CHAPTER 4
– Fort Sill Oklahoma – Artillery Survey School – December 1965-February 1966

Survey dates back to Ancient Egyptians—admirable!

I received a plane ticket and orders to report to Ft. Sill Oklahoma, for Survey School, after a two-week leave. The two weeks flew by and before I knew it I was boarding a Boeing 707 to Dallas Texas. From there I took a bus to one of the most desolate places I had ever seen, not including Alice Cramden's final resting place. But as usual, I got a little ahead of myself. I had enlisted in the Army with the thought of both serving my country and enhancing my résumé for a civilian career as a surveyor—and had chosen that as my Army Military Occupational Skill (MOS), accordingly. This would allow me to follow in the footsteps of young George Washington, who parlayed his surveying experience into the rank of an officer and scout in the British Army during the French and Indian War, leading inexorably to the Presidency.* While I

---

*The British commissioned Washington a Colonel in the militia of the British "Province of Virginia" during the French and Indian War. Having had some experience in skirmishes with the enemy, Washington told the British commander, Major-General Edward Braddock, of the tactics the French and Indians would employ. Failing to heed his warning, the British were nearly annihilated as they were ambushed by a hailstorm of fire loosed from behind cover. Washington assumed command of a rear guard, which allowed the remnants of the British forces to retreat to safety. As he did throughout the war, Washington exposed himself to withering enemy fire, in order to rally the forces under him. Amazingly, he had two horses shot out from under him and escaped the four musket balls that tore through his clothes—without a scratch!

had no such lofty aspirations, a job in the outdoors—particularly one that didn't require standing in line or marching—would do nicely.

I should have read the fine print, as I was soon to discover that I was to be schooled in "Field Artillery" survey, rather than the type used by the Army Corps of Engineers, which was more closely aligned with the type of survey required for construction and related projects. The difference being that the equipment and training for field artillery survey resulted in an accuracy of no better than 1 in 500 (as in one foot for every 500), whereas the Engineers' surveys required an accuracy of 1 in 25,000. In comparison to the Artillery Survey, the Egyptians built the pyramids to a greater degree of accuracy 5,000 years ago.

If you're wondering why the Army allowed, even promoted, such carelessness regarding the time-honored profession of survey, the answer can be found in the accuracy of the weaponry that would utilize the survey. For example, a shell fired by a 105mm Howitzer at the maximum range of 11,500 meters, could still hit a target within its kill radius, based on a 1 and 500 error factor. Therefore, there wasn't a need for a more accurate survey. In fact, since the kill radius of the Howitzer shell was nearly 100 meters, enemy soldiers, not even targeted, would still be eligible to answer George C. Scott's stirring call to arms, immortalized in his opening dialogue in his Oscar-winning performance in the acclaimed 1970's movie, *Patton*.

Unfortunately, I didn't plan on employing 105 mm Howitzers when I became a civilian, and accuracy of the survey equipment I was to learn to use would only result in property disputes. And I had no plans to augment my salary by becoming a lawyer. After realizing I had made a drastic error in carelessly opting for just "Survey," without specifying that I wanted to do a little better than the ancient Egyptians, I decided to make the best of it—by getting out of survey all together.* Thinking there might be a career in aviation, I put in for Warrant Officers Flight School to learn to fly helicopters. I passed all the tests with flying colors, except the one involving *colors*. It turned out that, like many men, I was partially color blind, a malady which was fatal to my desire to learn another skill that might prove useful in civilian life.

Turning to another choice, I signed up for "Leader Preparation School" (LPS), a two-week course that would prove to be a stepping-stone to Officer's Candidate School (OCS), which would result in becoming a second lieutenant. However, this would cause me to miss the current training cycle, which was fine with me. The two weeks were basically a crash course in the rudiments of becoming an NCO and I did quite well in the first step of my intended entry into the OCS program as I was appointed the "Platoon Guide" of the next class. The symbol of this new-found position was a sleeve with sergeant stripes that slipped over my stripeless shirt sleeve. The ersatz stripes signaled that I had the rank of SFC (Sergeant First Class) and charge over about 60 soldiers which comprised the survey class.

While enjoying the momentary privilege of that rank, which included my own room, I still had to learn the same skills everyone else did, which eventually became the undoing of my plans. The event that proved fatal to my acceptance

---

*The main instruments used in artillery survey consisted of a T-15 Theodolite, a 30-meter measuring tape, range poles, a plumb bob, and pins (used when measuring distance on a slope). The survey squad had seven members—an instrument operator, a recorder who recorded the readings and paced the distance between two stations (as a check), two tapers, and two computation men who converted the angles and measurements into map coordinates, and of course, their fearless leader, which was to become me.

into OCS occurred during the last week of actual survey training and had nothing to do with the technical aspects of survey—in which I was very proficient. I suspect that my downfall had to do with a practical joke I pulled on the unit's first sergeant, who apparently had no sense of humor.

Since the new class wasn't going to start Christmas week, I was given a pass to go home for Christmas but had to prove I had purchased a round trip ticket (airline or bus) home. Thinking I'd get home a lot faster and save the bus fare, I hitch-hiked to Dallas in the belief that a soldier in uniform could be able to get a stand-by seat on a commercial carrier. Big mistake. When I got to the airport, I found hundreds of other GI's had the same idea, and the airlines were overbooked, to boot. Luckily, I had enough time to get back to the bus depot in Lawton and catch a Greyhound bus with the ticket I'd bought, and still make it home in time to catch Santa coming down the chimney.

So, my now large capacity bladder and I settled in for a two-day bus trip, with a stopover in St. Louis, Missouri. I recall playing Nat King Cole's *A Christmas Song*, again and again, while I got drunk in a bar in the bus station, while dreaming of getting home to see my girlfriend on Christmas Eve. Unfortunately, taking a bus back to Fort Sill required me to leave the day after Christmas, giving me only one full day home and four days of travel.

Since I would have to start the return trip almost as soon as I got home, I wondered if there was some way to get the five-day pass extended. I got the answer from an orderly at the now-closed Fort Totten Army Base just across the White Stone Bridge from my home in the Bronx. It seemed that all I had to do was return to any Army post before my leave was up, with a good excuse for not having a means to return to my home base on time— like "I was kidnapped by aliens"— and I would not be considered AWOL. This meant I could stay home an extra two days. And the best part was, after calling my home base, the duty officer at Fort Totten told me to go home until the Army could arrange for an airline ticket for my return to Fort Sill. And since all the air lines were sold out, I got to stay home another week. My good luck got even better when I learned that the new Leader Preparation School cycle was to begin after the New Year, which meant my extended leave wouldn't result in any disruption to my plan to enter the OCS program.

Let me digress here to tell you a little about the history of Fort Sill. It was originally a few adobe buildings set up as a re-supply post in 1869 for six cavalry regiments, including the famous "7th Cav," which had come west to deal with a group of Indian tribes who were terrorizing the settlers in the region. These units were under the command of none other than General William Tecumseh Sherman, who oversaw what became known as the Indian Wars. Sherman named the fort after General Joshua W. Sill who had been killed in the Civil War. The combatants included several Indian tribes led by the famed Indian Chief Geronimo. The cavalry units were accompanied by scouts, including Wild Bill Hickok and Buffalo Bill Cody. After the hostilities ended, Geronimo was permitted to accompany Cody on his touring Wild West Show, which became famous throughout the world.

Before you get too taken with the Fort's noted early history, let me draw a picture of the Fort Sill area for you. You can do it yourself; just turn a sheet of paper sideways and draw a horizontal line from one side to the other. To be more accurate, make the line slightly convex, to represent the horizon, because that is how far you could see. There's an old joke about the area being so flat that you could see your dog for three days after it ran away.

And you don't have to take my word for it—included in the photo collection in the back of this book is a photo of me setting up a survey instrument in an open area. If you look carefully, you may still see the dog that took it on the lam. Topographers would describe the land as lacking in "relief," a *term of art* meaning the land was flat. There were other things lacking in relief including relief from the heat, dust and boredom. However, there was the nearby town of Lawton which offered the type of diversion that most towns have who owe their existence to a nearby Army base. (More about Lawton in a minute.)

After completing the LPS cycle, I took command of the survey class the first week, which was just centered on book learning. We studied the rudiments of map reading and the map coordinate system.

For those to whom the term is foreign, an example would be that New York City (NYC) is approximately 40 degrees north longitude and 74 degrees west latitude (abbreviated *40 N* and *74 W*). Think of latitude as imaginary parallel lines which slice the earth in half, starting at the equator, which is at zero degrees. A slice taken at 40 degrees North latitude would dissect NYC. The North Pole is the top of the Earth and 90 degrees above the Equator; the South Pole is 90 degrees south of the equator.

While my editor wanted to delete this discussion, since the advent of GPS (Global Positioning System) had rendered it boring to most, I told him that I wasn't worried, as the book probably wouldn't sell anyway. Besides, the details are needed to explain how it's possible to be in two places at once. I bet that perked up your interest; didn't it?

Distances east and west are measured in lines of longitude which meet at the poles, with zero degrees being the location of the Prime Meridian, which passes through England. A location at 180 degrees would be the opposite side of the earth, and is known as the International Date Line (IDL).

Locations in between would be so many degrees east or

west of the Prime Meridian. This 180-degree imaginary line zigzags around Islands to avoid the inhabitants from on one side of an island from celebrating holidays on a different day than the other. Although, this would give them the opportunity to celebrate holidays twice, by simply crossing the street. Contrary to popular belief, this would also allow someone to be in two places at the same time.

This amazing feat could be accomplished by simply straddling the IDL. One half of the of the person would be at 179 degrees, 59 minutes and 59 seconds west, and the other half the same reading *east* of the IDL.

We also studied the principles of the surveying. Which basically involved extending the above-discussed map coordinates from a known location to an unknown location. Neglecting altitude, this required two things, measuring changes in direction and distance.

Direction was determined by reading an angle, in mils (rather than hours, minutes and seconds) between a known point, such as a church steeple, to the new location. The process started by leveling the instrument's Vernier plate directly over the starting point of known coordinates. A sighting was then taken on a distant object of known direction, which would be the base line. The instrument would then be sighted on the new location—or "station" as it was called—and the angle between the prior station and the new one recorded.

Distance between the location with known coordinates and the new station was measured with a 30-meter steel tape. Once the physical data had been recorded, it was used to compute the new station's coordinates (longitude and latitude) using trigonometric functions and ephemeris tables to interpolate fractions and, if I recall, compensate for the curvature of the earth.

An example of the above process would look like this. If the known or starting location were NYC (40 N and 74 W) and a sighting were taken due east, which we'll assume is zero for this example, and the new location was sighted at 180 mils or due west of NYC and 69 Miles distant,* the coordinates of the new location would 40 N and 75 W. If this all seems a bit confusing, not to worry, as GPS (Global Positioning System) has eliminated the need to do any of this anyway.

There were a few events that are worth the retelling here. The first involves a cheap trick played on us by our instructor. Back in the mid-sixties, surveys were still run the old-fashioned way, *i.e.*, by measuring distances with a 30-meter (approximately 98 feet) steel tape. This required a team of two soldiers, a lead man who would stick a pin in the ground at the front end, and a following soldier, who would retrieve the rear pin as the team moved along. The distance was checked off one tape length at a time.

When measuring distances between stations the instrument operator and recorder were instructed to pace the distance as they went, as a double check of the taped distances.

Our field training involved determining the coordinates of a station, via a series of traverse legs starting from a point of known coordinates and direction. Since we first set up on a station with known coordinates and a given direction to a landmark, the results of our completed survey should have yielded the pre-determined coordinates of the final station we were to close the survey upon.

Unfortunately, after completing the survey the first day, the final coordinates we calculated did not agree with the ones noted on that final station.

Since the survey did close on direction, we knew the error

---

*1 degree of arc at the equator is equal to approximately 69 miles (360 mils x 69.169 miles = 24,901 miles, which is the earth's circumference at the equator.)

had to be in either the computations* or in the distance measuring. Since the computations were done independently by two men, using the data given them by the instrument operator and taping team, the possibility that both had made the same error was remote. Since we could not leave the area until the survey closed, we were forced to re-measure the distances between each station.

After cursing out the two "morons"—who had so carelessly done the taping—and the recorder who followed the instrument operator—whose job it was to pace off the distances between the legs of the survey—we figured the quickest way to discover the error was to use a another pair of legs to pace off the distances between the stations. And that seemed promising as we discovered an apparent error in length of the first station checked between the paced and taped distance.

Unfortunately, when we re-taped that leg, the recorded measurement checked out. Since the paced distances could not be relied on to detect small errors, we were forced to re-tape every leg of the survey, one at a time in hopes of finding the apparent errors quickly. However, after carefully re-

---

*I'm reminded that our current blind reliance on electronic devices such as digital watches, calculators and the like can result in our making major errors, as we have surrendered our problem-solving ability to machines. When I went to college, the slide rule, a kind of precision calibrated ruler with multiple sliding sections, was used to solve complex math problems, such as square roots. The user had to know the magnitude of the answer being sought, as an answer of 25,000 is located at the same crossing lines as 2,500. Since the advent of the GPS we have lost our ability to estimate direction from the sun, digital watches have robbed us of our perspective of time, and the use of the calculator has all but eliminated our sense of the magnitude of numbers. As a result of our reliance on instruments' brains, it is possible for Santa's helpers to mistake an order for 600 one-foot toy soldiers with 100 six-foot ones, as happened to the toymaker who employed Stan Laurel and Oliver Hardy, in the classic 1930's movie *Babes in Toyland*.

measuring each leg, which differed from the distances paced, we were still unable find the error(s).

It had become dark as we re-measured each station, forcing us to re-tape the final legs using flashlights. Now thoroughly stumped and having exhausted every expletive learned from our drill instructors—which were directed at each other, the Army, and the survey gods—we notified our instructor that we were unable to "close" the survey, despite super-human effort. He didn't have much sympathy for our dilemma and suggested he would be happy to approve transfers to the infantry or the less demanding field artillery units, which were inhabited by those individuals euphemistically known to us as the "gun bunnies."

Running out of options, I had the brilliant thought that maybe there was something amiss in the tape we were using. (*How easily our memories allow us to take credit for things!*) Laying our tape on flat ground, each of us took turns pacing the distance. We soon realized that something was rotten in Denmark and we began to examine the tape one centimeter at a time. At the 15-meter mark, we discovered that the number 16 was missing. It was clear that someone had skillfully removed one meter from the center of the tape, thereby causing each 30 meters to actually measure only 29 meters in length. When the adjustments were made to our calculations, low and behold, the survey closed, *i.e.*, the coordinates agreed.

Wishing to get even with the instructor, we advised him that we had successfully closed the survey. Moreover, after carefully taping each leg of the traverse twice we had discovered that some prankster had moved the last station, but he'd be glad to know that we moved it back to its correct location.

While we enjoyed learning a few new Army expletives, we decided that discretion was the better part of valor and told him we had not actually moved the monument but discovered that some "jackass" had removed a meter from the tape without making the requisite mark on the ends noting the tape had been repaired. We didn't tell another soul about this tape (*Why spoil anyone else's fun?*) and I gave up wondering how many hapless "morons" fell into the same trap. However, I have a vivid memory of how the attitude of our instructor changed towards me, following this event, as it may well have saved my life— although I doubt that was his intention, at the time.

There are two other non-training related events I recall that might be of a bit of interest. The first involves something I observed first-hand that I'd once heard about and doubted was true. It's gross, but then today's society norms have changed the meaning of the word, and things once considered as such are now a comedy movie staple. Anyway, don't let anyone tell you that flatulence is not highly flammable. One night we were gabbing about what to do with someone who let go with a couple without fair warning to the bystanders. One of the guys volunteered that we could learn who the guilty party was by tossing a match at the backside of the most likely suspect, next time it happened as this would result in a self-incriminating flare-up. When most of us doubted this was possible, we were given a demonstration. And the flame that evinced from the GI as he let one go near a flicked Zippo lighter resembled a mini flamethrower, I kid you not. Perhaps this is what gave rise to the limerick about the man from Boston Mass. I'm also reminded of the British saying that the world is populated by two kinds of assholes. The first being considered an ordinary "arsehole," and other being characterized as a "flaming" one.

Using the art of segue and the fact that Army chow was known to produce an abundance of fuel for use as an afterburner, another memorable detail about Ft. Sill came via chili hamburgers served at a hash-house in the nearby town of Lawton, which had sprung up once the Army base grew of a size to support bars and related industries. Meaning no offense to the fine citizens of the town, the most prosperous industry back then was laundering the GI's dirty clothes and, some say, their wallets as well. Anyhow, the hamburger bun was worthy of a cattle town, as it was the size of a medium sized pizza and contained well over a pound of beef and chili. No exaggeration. You needed hands large enough to palm a basketball to hold on to it and an appetite to match. There were even some adjoining cut-rate rooms, where you could sleep it off, if you managed to eat a whole one, without taking at least one pit stop at some point.

Back to the training . . . As the Platoon Guide for the survey class, I had certain responsibilities, such as the wake-up call, lights-out enforcement, and formations. I also called cadence when marching, which I thoroughly enjoyed. Not sure why, but there seems to be some primordial attachment for men to march together in unison. I'm sure you've seen movies of parading soldiers, military marching bands, and possibly the precision of the US Marines Drill Team demonstrating the manual of arms. If not, check out the opening credits of the movie *A Few Good Men*.

One observation about the subject: while marching and engaging enemy forces in structured formation dates to the Sumerian and Egyptian civilizations, it now has only training and ceremonial value. In fact, the Army discourages non-training or related marching in step, which can damage a bridge, as a large group of men marching in unison can set up a harmonic motion which could cause a bridge to sway from side to side. The command to cease marching in unison and to spread out a bit is called "route step." And, while there's an old cliché about safety in numbers, it hasn't fared well following a disputed call at an international soccer match.

I was also responsible for the non-technical aspects of the training, including study habits, tutoring, administering, and marking test papers. Unbeknownst to me at the time, this last item was to have a marked effect on my future in the service and probably the remainder of my life, as well. One of my friends in the unit, Mike Poster, was from Montana. I called him Montana Mike, for some reason. Mike was not in the regular Army but had enlisted in the National Guard (NG), and his active duty would end upon graduation. Thereafter, his military commitment would involve dressing in his Army uniform and reporting to an NG station one weekend a month, plus a two-week training stint, each year.

Since I was familiar enough with the NG to know that he probably wouldn't be using much, if any, of the survey skills he was acquiring, I wasn't surprised that he didn't take the training as seriously as the rest of us. I had to keep after him to make sure he studied enough to graduate, since if he failed the final, he would have to repeat the entire two-month survey school training cycle.

When grading the final tests, I found that Mike had gotten something like a 63 and needed one more correct answer to get to the passing grade needed to avoid recycling with the next class. I corrected one of his obvious mistakes, which gave him a final passing grade, and thought no more about it. Our instructor must have found I'd changed an answer, as shortly thereafter I was called into the company commander's office, who proceeded to scream about my dishonoring myself and the Army by changing the grade of one of the men (*like doing so would have put lives at risk*).

When he stopped yelling in my face, I asked permission to speak candidly and explained that the soldier whose grade I'd changed was in the NG and, given the draft, it was extremely unlikely that he would ever be called up. And that I was satisfied that he could do the job, irrespective of one technical question he had screwed up on the final. My explanation only seemed to make the Captain angrier, and he told me I was being relieved of my temporary rank and he was going to reject my application for OCS, which he had on his desk and had been prepared to approve.

The next morning, our instructor seemed to take personal satisfaction in removing the temporary sergeant stripes from my sleeve in front of the formation, while announcing that I had been found unfit for the position. While wondering how I'd gotten caught, I was more bemused than embarrassed. If the charge had befallen a West Point, or even VMI cadet, I might have understood the reaction better. But adding a few points to a weekend warrior's training grade hardly seemed to warrant such a hullabaloo. I do, however, suspect our instructor might have laid it on thick when telling the commanding officer of my "crime," since I suspected he was looking for an opportunity to get even for my having called him a jackass, instead of a mule.

Two things resulted from this event. My stature among the trainees increased now that I was "one of the guys," and I lost a sure ticket to OCS, which turned out to be a blessing in disguise. I didn't realize this at the time but was to come to see it as such not long afterward.

Please forgive another sidebar here as the term "blessing in disguise" always reminds me of something one of the last century's greatest leaders once said to his wife, who used these same words to console him following the end of WWII, when he failed to win re-election as England's Prime Minister. This hero of mine, who authored 43 books, and created numerous highly sought-after paintings, responded to his wife's sympathetic words, "At the moment it seems quite *effectively* disguised."

The speaker, for all those who are destined to repeat history, was Winston Churchill—whose mother, by the way, was an American. This leads me to mention a word about the long-standing connection between America and Great Britain.

I always liked how George C. Scott, characterized it in his seminal role as General George C. Patton as "two countries separated by a common language." Funny, how these words now seem to define the state of interaction, or more accurately the lack thereof, in our own country.

The next event I recall was graduation day. We all gathered around as our orders for our next assignment were read aloud. It seemed that many of the graduates had received orders to go to Viet Nam, while some of us were being sent to other bases, some overseas. I learned my orders were to go to Munich, Germany. While I was happy about being sent to Germany, I could not help but wonder why so many surveyors were being sent to a country where the fighting was virtually all jungle warfare. When I asked how anyone could survey in a theater like that, I was told something along the lines "stupid, they are going to be Forward Observers."

While researching for this book, I read that the life expectancy of a Forward Observer (FO) in WWII was measured in hours, which might have been my fate had I been sent to Viet Nam, either as an FO or Second Lieutenant, as OCS grads were sure to go as well. In retrospect, I probably would not be writing this book had either of these assignments evinced. It seemed like some power greater than I had again intervened and saved me for another day.

If you're wondering how I felt about watching buddies go off to war while I was to be sent to Germany, at the time I was a bit ticked-off. Mainly because I had that sense of invincibility and desire to prove myself that only comes with the folly of youth. Only later, when learning how many of my fellow servicemen had been killed in the war, did I come to realize that I had probably been spared their fate. However, the greater honor I would have shared with those who served in a combat zone has not diminished the pride I feel for having answered my country's call, in a time of war. Having mastered the art of artillery survey, I was now prepared to grudgingly put it to good use. But before I had that opportunity, I found reason to be glad the Navy had rejected my enlistment papers . . .

CHAPTER 5
– Crossing the Atlantic – March 1966

Ocean voyages—not all they're cracked up to be

After graduating survey school, I was given a short leave before reporting to the Brooklyn Navy Yard in early March. There I was to board a WWII troop transport, the USNS Patch,* for a six-day voyage to Bremerhaven, Germany. Incidentally, I can attest to the fact that anyone who voluntarily makes an ocean voyage across the Atlantic in March, which is the stormy season, needs one of two things: The first is to have been raised by a flounder; the other is having the brain of one.

Fortunately, neither I nor any of the other 3,000 or so soldiers who boarded the troop transport in Brooklyn that year had an inkling of what awaited us once the Patch cleared the protection of the New York harbor. Had we foreseen what awaited us, the list of no-shows might have been as long as the shows. Once out in the open sea most of the troops spent the next six days searching, unsuccessfully, to find their sea legs — as the ship pitched and yawed every which way as it plowed through winter storms.

Kept below decks in cramped quarters, many who had

---

*While we have grown accustomed to public projects requiring years to complete, and wars that go on for decades, the generation that defeated the Axis Powers in less than four years, also constructed the largest office building in the world in 16 months (the Pentagon at 6.6 million square feet) and built thousands of "liberty ships" similar in size to the Patch in an average of 42 days. The record for building one was less than four days.

never been on a rowboat, never mind a ship, were too seasick to get out of the wall-to-wall bunks we were forced to spend virtually all our time in, except to eat or, more frequently, use the "head" (the Navy term for a steel-walled combination toilet and shower area with no dividing stalls). I witnessed more than a few soldiers simultaneously discharging the contents of their stomachs and bowls as they sat exposed on steel commodes while the ship imitated a bouncing football during an onside kick. To complete the scene, simply imagine the sound of a camel dying of the dry heaves.

Luckily, having grown up along the shores of Long Island Sound, I had some experience aboard boats during rough weather, and only experienced being seasick for brief periods. Because the weather was so rough, we were not permitted to go on deck. This probably saved the land lubbers from a far scarier scene—the sight of a storm on the high seas—as those who have braved even moderately heavy seas in a small boat can attest. I have been on open water when a sudden squall came up, and watched as waves began to rise and cap higher than the bow of the boat. I can assure you that it is a truly chilling and humbling experience. I've watched as the water, reflecting the darkening sky, turned black and menacing—and quickly realized that we were at the mercy of some gigantic force over which we had no control.

While on board, I somehow managed to get myself into one of the few fistfights I had while in the Army—which I vowed upon entry would never happen. I'd grown up in a tough environment and had more than my share of fights before joining the Army, and wanted to avoid repeating those errors, which had nearly cost me my freedom on a few occasions. Unfortunately, while you can take the boy out of the Bronx, you can't take the Bronx out of the boy. I had my first altercation while in basic training. Luckily, it was broken up before any serious punches were thrown. The one on the

Patch was worth the price of admission. I was standing in a chow line that extended more than a few decks, when a small group of privates began to pass us on the way down. My loathing of standing in a line caused me to step out and block their path. I told them to go to the end of the fucking line and wait their turn like the rest of us.

Not sure how it started, or even who threw the first punch, but after landing some heavy blows, I received a number in return from a well-built black dude. (I need to take a time out here to explain that I had grown up in Bronx housing projects and had many Black, Spanish, Irish and Jewish friends, and didn't know the meaning of the word prejudice. In fact, I had more than a few black friends in my units in Germany, at a time when racial tensions were running high. One of my black friends from Mount Vernon once said to me, "Nordstrom, you're just like a brother." (This is something that has always given me a great deal of pride.)

Since I had boxed a little with my older brother—he had a friend who was a professional fighter—I immediately realized this guy knew his way around a ring, and that I had my hands full. After exchanging a flurry of heavy blows, we were pulled apart—which neither of us seemed too upset about. I later noticed that our bunks were not far apart, but we looked at each other with mutual respect that signaled there would not be a return match.

As I recalled the details of that trip, it came to me that while onboard my 22nd birthday had passed, unnoticed by me at the time, as my thoughts were occupied elsewhere. The thought reminds of the dangers faced by the sailors who man our warships. On land, soldiers only have to face one enemy; at sea there are two.

On March 14, 1966 we finally arrived at the German port city of Bremerhaven—and after going through some paperwork (probably to confirm no one had been lost overboard or committed suicide), we were fed and given a place to sleep. The next day many of us were loaded onto a train bound for southern Germany (also known as Bavaria). About 100 of us detrained in Augsburg and, after more paperwork, were transferred to local bases. My Army records show that four days after landing in Bremerhaven, I was bused to a large Army base known as Henry *Kaserne* (German for "barracks"), located on the outskirts of Munich.

I heard that the Germans were particularly fond of American service men stationed in Berlin, because of its proximity to East Germany. As I think back to that time, I recall seeing a photo of President John F. Kennedy in every German home I would visit during the two-plus years I was stationed there. Many bore a caption of a famous line from a speech he gave standing beside the Berlin Wall in 1963: *"Ich bin ein Berliner."* What the American translator didn't know at the time was that the word *Berliner* was the local slang for "hot dog."

Berlin aside, I quickly learned that Munich was the best duty station in Germany for American soldiers. And I was on my way! ...

CHAPTER 6

– HHB 1st Battalion 34th Artillery - Henry Kaserne –
Munich Germany – March 1966

Elvis Presley slept here (?)

On March 18, 1966, I was assigned to the Survey Section of the Headquarters Battery, 1st Battalion, 35th Field Artillery (105 MM Howitzers), of the 24th Infantry Division. The unit was stationed in Henry Kaserne—which I learned was constructed prior to WWII for the German Army. As a private, I shared sleeping quarters with six other members of our survey squad. We each had our own foot-locker and wall-locker. The guys were friendly and showed me the ropes.

Our squad leader was a Specialist Fifth Class (Spec 5) named Greg Bridger. "Specialists" do not wear stripes on their uniforms like NCO's. Instead they wear a black cone-shaped patch: plain with no bars for the rank of Spec 4, with one curved bar atop the cone for Spec 5, two bars for Spec 6, etc. Spec 5 Bridger was as easygoing as anyone I encountered in the Army.

The survey section was headed by an NCO who was a bit of a by-the-rules "lifer" (the term enlisted men gave to career soldiers), who didn't like me—which I didn't do much to discourage, as the feeling was mutual. In fact, he lost a bet with Spec 5 Bridger that I would be kicked out of the NCO Academy I was to later attend. He was nearly right.

Being stationed in Munich was great, as the Munich downtown area was within easy reach on the *Straßenbahn* trolley car, which stopped not far from our Kaserne. And the downtown area was within walking distance of the Deutche Museum, Englese Gardens, outdoor dining areas, shops, and of course, the Hofbräuhaus (more about this beer hall a bit later). And if you wanted to get a snack or bottle of beer or wine after hours, there were coin operated dispensers built into the outside walls of buildings. While commonplace now, these self-serve stations were a novelty. The closest thing I recall to these was the Horn & Hardart Automats I'd frequented as a young man and later when I worked in New York City in the 1970's. They became an iconic part of New York and must-see tourist attraction until the last one closed in 1991. I guess it was the forerunner of the fast food burger and pancake palaces that permeate the landscape nowadays.

You will have to accept my apology regarding my next entry, as it is no longer fashionable to speak of prostitution given the current "Me-Too" movement, unless of course you're speaking about politicians. I'm broaching the subject because it was a fact of life (Army life, anyway) back then. Aside from the beer gardens, the GI's most frequented destination in Munich was a five-story apartment house a short distance from the more traditional tourist attractions. At this location a lonely or otherwise disposed GI, could purchase love by the hour, or part thereof. This was possible because a harem of young and desirable women stood outside apartment doors on every floor. That's what I heard, anyway.

This afforded GI's the one thing that all soldiers, sailors, and marines would agree is essential to their well-being—a supply of purchasable love. And, since I'm already on thin ice, I will add that I no longer see much difference between the Strasse queens, as they were called, and today's parade of ever more scantily clad women who expose their wares to sell every conceivable consumer product from automobiles to zucchini. I did a podcast show on this very subject.

As I was to discover in my new unit, there was one useable skill I possessed from civilian life that seemed to travel with my records. I had been a semi-skilled carpenter before enlisting, so I guess it was natural for me to "volunteer" my services to fix windows and doors when I was in basic training. One of our drill instructors even volunteered me to build a doghouse. This facility resulted in my being assigned other "outside the lines" projects someone thought I could do better than most, including painting the 24th Division's insignia* on an assembly area block wall.

The Insignia was given to the division when it was formed during WWII from a disbanded Hawaiian Division, hence the Taro Leaf patch. The 24th saw significant action in the Pacific during WWII and served as an occupation force in Japan following the war. Because of its location, it was the first unit to see action during the Korean War.

In addition to becoming the unit's Mr. Fixit, and given the Army's unfailing logic, it follows that anyone who could drive a nail must be able to drive a truck. This is the only rational I can come up with to explain why I was assigned as a designated driver for groups of "aggressors" who were dispatched to harass units during training exercises. I didn't mind these assignments at all as it kept me from pulling KP and Guard Duty, as well as away from the watchful eye of our fearless leader.

On one of the sorties the sergeant in charge told me to "Step on it," because the squad was running late and might not be able to fully harass the "enemy," as planned. As I rounded a corner, I discovered that Army vehicles are not designed to be driven at more than 20 miles per hour. As a re-

---

* The Insignia was circular in design with a large green taro leaf centered in a field of red. The patch was fringed in green and the taro leaf was outlined in yellow. The replica I attempted was about three feet in diameter and made by painstakingly scaling the actual patch configuration. While the circle was round enough the finished product was a bit distorted and could have passed for a Salvador Dali knock-off.

sult, the outside wheels of the 3/4-ton truck I was driving came completely free of the road, scaring the shit out of everyone on board, me most of all. And even though I immediately got the truck back on its four wheels, the sergeant in charge proceeded to rip me a new one. Even though I thought the event proved I was an exceptional driver, I was never again assigned to transport duty.

Fate was to deal me another winning hand, as this very same sergeant would later play a role in my taking first place in a vehicle driving contest, though I'm sure that wasn't his intent. Perhaps the fact that I had made a turn on two wheels was taken as a positive, as someone in my unit decided I should represent the company's colors at an annual Division level driving contest known as a "rodeo." When I saw that the aforementioned sergeant was also grading the contest, I thought my goose was cooked.*

Thinking I had nothing to lose, I drove my 3/4-ton truck through the twisting, cone-laden obstacle course in forward and reverse without disturbing a single obstacle, and in the fastest time recorded. Other components of the competition included general vehicle knowledge and maintenance. At the conclusion of the Rodeo, I walked over to the presiding captain and told him that the grading sergeant might have an axe to grind with me, and the reason for it. How much this played a role in the final decision, I'll never know, but I was awarded first prize, which consisted of a certificate and trophy of a tire with wings on the sides, upon which was inscribed my name and that of my unit, along with the date. The reason I'm telling you this story is I believe this played a part in a streak of good fortune that included my being quickly promoted

---

* If the reader is interested, the expression apparently comes from the burning of Jan Hus, a 14th century Czech priest, whose last name sounded like the word Goose in Czechian.

through the ranks and more importantly, to my taking home the ultimate prize, the wonderful woman who agreed to be my wife only four months later. But meanwhile I would learn that "camping out" would take on a whole new meaning . . .

CHAPTER 7

– Grafenwöhr, Germany Training Center
– April 1966

Fast Cars, Howitzers, and the Black Market.

About a month after I arrived, our unit moved out for a training exercise in Grafenwöhr or "Graf" as we called it. Graf was a very large training area (approximately 150 square miles) in the Bavarian Alps. Its seclusion and topography made it ideal for live fire exercises conducted by American and German forces, as well as those by neighboring NATO Allies. Graf contained a very large open valley with a lake at its center, and was ringed by mountains—which made it ideal for live artillery and tank fire. The floor of the Valley was loaded with old tanks, trucks and such, which were used as targets— periodically replenished when no longer recognizable.

Our unit traveled to Grafenwöhr via one of the six-lane super-highways known as *Autobahns*. These were constructed by the Germans prior to WWII and built to withstand heavy military equipment. While we moved at a snail's pace, there was no speed limit on the Autobahn, and cars continually sped by us at speeds exceeding 100 MPH. Many of these cars were equipped with banks of headlights mounted on the front grill and a very loud horn, both of which would be fully employed when a driver encountered a slower vehicle in the passing lane. It's unfortunate that options like this are illegal in the good old US of A, as I'm sure we've all been stuck behind a "Good Samaritan" who believes it's their duty to enforce the speed limit. Ever notice how they will suddenly accelerate when you try to pass them on the right? I guess it's

OK for them to speed for a good cause.

As a result of the roads being simultaneously occupied by cars traveling in excess of 100 miles per hour and much slower ones like the 1956 Volkswagen I was soon to acquire, accidents were all too common. This led to one of the first expressions I learned in German, besides *Wir ghet's, Shatzie?* (How's it going sweetheart?). The expression was *"Ich bin ein Unfall passiert"* (I've had an accident). Followed by *"Wo ist eine Krankenhaus?"* (Where is a hospital?) The gallows humor joke we passed around was that Germans and their super-fast cars were inseparable, and at speeds over 100 MPH, they were generally buried that way.

When we moved into Graf the unit quickly set up its command post and other sections. The job of our survey section was to bring control (map coordinates) to a location where our artillery unit was to be set up. We would then establish observation posts (OP's) to direct the fire and report on its accuracy. The coordinates of the artillery battery's location and estimated map coordinates of a target were called into the Fire Control Center (FDC), which would then calculate the firing data (direction, elevation, size and type of shell and powder to be used) for the artillery battery. The wind direction and strength and even temperature were variables that had to be considered as well.

The object of the observer (as with a forward observer in combat) was to find the range to a target by calling for a single shell to be fired "long" (past a target) and when that was done, the FO would call for a round to be fired short, so as to "box" the target. Same with side-to-side location. As an example, if a round was long and off to one side of the target, the FO would then overcorrect and might call "down 200, right 100" (as in meters). If that round fell short but in line with the target, then the command might be "Up 100. Fire for effect" would result in the entire battery unleashing a barrage until the call to "Cease fire" was given.

A bit more about the make-up of our section—it was divided into two squads; each one consisting of up to a seven-man team. Each team included a squad leader, an instrument operator and recorder, two tapers who measured distances, and two of those members who would also calculate the coordinates of the new stations, based on the collected raw data. The main job of the squad leader was to choose the route the team would "traverse" to extend control from a known location to the one chosen for setting up the artillery.

Since the starting and ending locations were usually some distance apart, temporary intermediate stations had to be set up, which had to be in line of sight of each other. The squad leader chose these intermediate locations based on the topography of the area and other factors, but experience and common sense were most important. The intermediate stations were typically marked by a wooden stake driven into the ground, upon which a tripod and "Range Pole" were set. Once the starting point and the first intermediate station were set up, the survey would begin.

As soon as the map coordinates of the end station were determined, the information was relayed to the FDC section, who would then go about determining the information required to direct the artillery fire. The whole idea was to accurately lay down artillery fire on the enemy, hopefully before they could return the favor. And it goes without saying that, until you know with some degree of accuracy where you are and where the enemy is, the 105 MM gunners won't know which way to point their guns. (It was OK to call the artillery pieces "guns" as they were too heavy to run around with over our heads).

By the way, anyone who took trigonometry in high school will appreciate the fact that converting the horizontal distances measured on a long traverse survey had to take into account the fact the earth isn't flat, although some still cling to the belief that it is, despite Columbus having proved otherwise over 500 years ago. That group may have found new footing, given the newest addition to the catalogue of oxymorons, *i.e.*, our "institutes of higher learning." Pardon a humble observation here, but it seems that colleges that once practiced the art of teaching students how to use their own brains are now trying their hardest to protect them from the traumatic experience of doing so.*

Back to our story. Since I was new to the outfit, I wasn't expected to do much at Graf and don't recall much beyond sleeping in a place without a roof or a bed and eating canned meals that were generally left-over WWII C-rations—like cans of pork roast loaded with chemicals. The neat thing about the C-Ration cans is they fit snugly in the spaces between the exhaust manifold pipes or our 3/4-ton truck engine block. This provided us with a hot meal. And, if we were really unlucky, we got to eat with the unit at a field kitchen. And we didn't have to open any C-Rations, as they were already opened for us and were served as an Oriental delicacy "Goo-Who over rice."

We actually grew accustomed to dining on WWII C-rations, as they were regularly served to us at our home base and also when we were on maneuvers. Since the C-Rations we were eating were date stamped in the mid-1940's, I wondered if our unit was part of an experiment to test whether the contents were actually still edible up to the 20-year expiration date stamped on the side of the cases. The food wasn't as bad as this may sound, given the fact that the regular Army chow wasn't something to write home about either. As Victor

---

* I did a podcast show on this subject on which I interviewed the ghost of Albert Einstein (replete with German accent) in September of 2017. It was so popular he came back for an encore!

Hugo once observed, "Hunger is the gravy of the masses."

The other WWII vestiges we grew accustomed to were the vehicles we drove, including my favorite, the always reliable Willis WWII "jeep." The word was derived from the Army's designating it a "general purpose" (GP) Vehicle. The other vehicles which saw the most service in our unit were the 3/4-ton truck and the so-called "Deuce and a Half," a large all duty truck with a carrying capacity of two and a half tons. The thing all three had in common were high ground clearance, four-wheel drive, fold-down front windshields and canvas covered truck beds. The jeep had no doors or windows, but could be fitted with a canvas covered frame with a top, side curtains, and doors for use in cold weather.

The other great thing about the Army trucks is that many had winches on the front—which allowed us to pull them out of places we managed to get them stuck in. This was important, as whenever we had a chance we'd test them to see how deep into a swamp (or snow drift) we could plow before we needed to be winched out. We'd also drive up the steepest hills we could find and only back off when the front tires started to come off the ground. This was akin to the practice rounds a professional golfer takes to learn how their clubs played, as well as the nuances of the courses they planned to play on. Since our survey section considered itself on a par with other professionals, and given that we were often out on our own, we had plenty of opportunities to put the jeep through its paces, with the aim of making the Baja Test Trials look like a rubber ducky in an America's Cup yacht race.

There was only one serious drawback about driving WWII vehicles in the mid-60's. They often broke down and were out of commission until the spare parts arrived. Since we had to inspect our vehicles every day when in camp, the process became farcical, particularly when a truck was down waiting for spare parts. It was like doing an EKG on a dead body. We found all sorts of ways to deal with the monotony, including climbing under a truck with a grease gun to take a nap or letting air out of a tire so it could be inflated to the proper pressure. This daily routine was called "motor stables," a term which recalls the days when Army vehicles were the one-horsepower type. I wonder if the horse soldiers of yore, ("cavalry") also had to monitor the intake and exhaust manifolds of their horses on a daily basis.

There were a few other issues that resulted from using WWII vintage vehicles. The first and most important was the fact that the scarcity of spare parts at times affected the combat readiness of the unit. I'm sure this had more than a bit to do with the war in Viet Nam taking priority. But the Army addressed this problem by insuring that we could pass the frequent unannounced Inspections General (IG) review of our unit's readiness via a logistical sleight of hand. Thus, the combat effectiveness of our unit was confirmed, if only on paper. For example, a jeep that couldn't be started because it needed a carburetor was deemed logistically fit for duty if the order for the replacement part was proper and duly recorded in the jeep's logbook—something every vehicle had.

The logbook was a type of diary of the vehicle's service record. It included a complete listing of all repairs done and parts replaced, with the mileage and dates of same. It also contained a record of each time the vehicle was driven somewhere, including the destination, date, time, mileage, and purpose of use.

It became a running joke that if the enemy ever attacked, they would be forced to yield the field to our superior record keeping. One of the more comical moments in the saga of the spare parts occurred when it began to rain and a guy in our unit hung a spare parts order tag for missing wiper blades in front of the windshield of his truck—which flapped back and forth as he drove.

In the Army's defense, the public should understand that the protocol for replacement parts was driven in part by the its tireless effort to ensure that the taxpayer's money was carefully spent, via the use of algorithms to determine how many spare parts a unit needed to have on hand. Thus, the number and type of carburetors, tires, mufflers, etc. that each unit could keep as spares was subject to a type of actuary table. The logic was intended to prevent a unit from stockpiling unneeded spare parts, depriving other units of spare parts at a critical time.

The problem with the calculations was that they seemed to be based on some historical table—without accounting for the conditions the vehicle was operated in, and sporadic heavy usage. Thereafter, once a unit had all the spare parts it was calculated to require, it could only get new ones by returning the worn-out ones.

But if GI's were nothing else, they were highly creative in solving problems like this. Particularly if it meant getting over on the Army—which was often looked upon as the enemy until such time as there was a real one. And there was another problem to overcome: In addition to not having spare parts when they were needed, a unit couldn't have more than was allocated. If an unannounced Inspectors General inspection found a unit had overstocked spare parts, the result could involve serious consequences. In the Army's logic, having too many spare parts was the same as stealing from another unit.

Not to worry, as the good old American system of free enterprise saved the day. It came in the form of a sort of after-hour spare parts market where the motor pool could obtain all the spare parts it wanted by supplying the vehicle parts suppliers with something they wanted, like steaks and cases of C-Rations. And how did the motor pool guys come by such valuable commodities, you ask? From the mess hall, of course. (And how did they do this without sacrificing the health of the unit you ask? Hold that thought, and I'll get to it in a minute.) So, while the Army kept close tabs on all of the new parts, they didn't bother to keep records on the returned ones. Thus, the black market in new parts was actually one in *used* parts that could be *exchanged* for new ones.

By the way, I read an article some time ago that the people who lived under the former Soviet Union (now under a dictatorship), were just as creative as we were when it came to overcoming government regulations. This included the quantity of strategic consumables Citizen Ivan was allotted, such as light bulbs. While high ranking party officials apparently had access to all the light bulbs they wanted, the only way for Ivan could get a new light bulb was to turn in a burnt out one. And the scarcity of light bulbs might explain the popularity of Vodka over the collected works of Vladimir Lenin. Like us, the Russians resolved their problem via a black market—in their case, in burnt out light bulbs.

As a postscript, this is the reason we should insist on having old parts returned to us once a repair is completed—to prevent nefarious repair shops from simply cleaning up and reinstalling our own parts while showing us really worn out parts kept for that purpose.

Back to the Army. Having overcome the problem of a lack of handy spare parts to keep our vehicles operating, we now had to contend with surprise inspections, which included inventorying the quantity of spare parts allocated to a unit. Fortunately, the motor pool guys had an antidote: The smaller spare parts were kept on ice by the mess hall guys, who didn't want to lose liberty—or meet an even worse fate if a unit were found to have violated the spare parts regulations. While storing parts in the mess hall's freezers solved this problem, it produced another one, as the empty boxes of frozen string beans that were used could result in the cooks serving timing belt *au jus* in lieu of string beans *au gratin*. After all, cooks can't be expected to recognize a timing belt, even though most had been auto mechanics in private life.

The bigger spare parts—like mufflers, tailpipes, and tires—while easier for the cooks to recognize, could not be as easily stored in a freezer, or camouflaged as an *object d'art*. So they had to be stored where they could be quickly disposed of, at the first sign of a surprise inspection. Strategic disposal points included temporary storage in an adjoining unit's dumpsters or the ever-available fence line that surrounded the Kaserne, which quickly led to another cottage industry; one managed by the local Germans.

You may be still wondering where the excess steaks and cases of C-Rations came from, as alluded to above. Well, it derived, again, from the Army's use of careful calculations of the quantity of foodstuffs assigned to each unit, although a working knowledge of advanced calculus wasn't needed in this case. Food supplies for the mess halls were allocated based on a weekly tally of the number of meals served during the prior week.

The problem with this system was that GI's would blow their monthly pay off-base, shortly after receiving it, and didn't eat in the mess hall until the money ran out. As a result, the mess sergeant would have to order, and somehow dispose of, the over-order of fresh food and C-Ration allocation the week following the pay period. This was done so there would be enough food delivered to feed the hungry troops the week following.

And, where did the excess food go, when not needed for barter? *Voilá*, another windfall for the private sanitation companies that picked up the dumpsters! And, given the maxim that one man's jetsam is another's livelihood, it's quite possible that the knowledge of this dumpster largess played a part in some industrious German company's low garbage removal bid. The consolation is that the Army may have recouped ten cents on the dollar, or maybe twenty, if one considers a lower garbage removal bid as the product of the Army's spare parts and food allocation protocols.

Not sure how I got so far afield here, but such was life for those of us lucky enough in 1966 to be worried about inspections, while other far worthier souls were worried about something infinitely more serious, *i.e.*, a bullet with their name on it, as the ill-fated war in Viet Nam raged on. This realization was with me every day I sat down to write this book. However, in response to those who would gainsay my writing a comedy about my time in the service, my response is I believe I did my duty to my country when I enlisted without any strings. In fact, had I not been color blind, or unfairly (I believed) denied admission to OCS, I would have been guaranteed at least one tour in Viet Nam as either a helicopter pilot or second lieutenant.

The tragedy of this misbegotten war lingers today in scared bodies and minds of the soldiers (and their families) who fought valiantly, only to greeted with disdain, after losing the war, despite winning every battle.

I've grown philosophical about the unfairness of it all, and to borrow a phrase from M. Scott Peck's *The Road Less Traveled*, albeit with my own twist, life is neither fair nor unfair, it's simply life. Dr. Peck said it a bit differently (paraphrasing): "Life is difficult—once we accept that fact, it is no longer difficult—it is simply life." The profoundness of this truth requires nothing further from me.

I suspect that, by now, you are either growing accustomed to my meandering off the main topic or growing more impatient with the interruptions. The habit of making reflective detours has been with me throughout my life. I hope that, in balance, they have not been too distracting, and maybe even added to your enjoyment of the book.

Resuming the main story: After returning to the daily routine in Henry Kaserne, I began to see the advantage of married life for those lucky enough to have their wives living with them. Married soldiers could be assigned "Government Quarters" off base, which turned out to be very comfortably appointed apartments in housing complexes rented from the Germans. Once assigned to this housing, Army life became a quasi-civilian six-to-four job.

Since I was deeply in love with my future wife Susan, I commenced a campaign to convince her that she would love to live with me in Germany. This came to pass, not many months later. Because two people could not possibly live on a private's pay, I was lucky to be promoted to PFC E-3 (Private First Class) on May 21, 1966. While only involving a modest increase in my monthly pay, it was an extremely important step to the next pay grade of E-4, in my case Spec-4, which would be needed if I hoped to marry Sue and bring her to live with me in Germany. I was promoted to Spec-4 only four months later, and soon I was reaching for that gold ring . . .

CHAPTER 8
– Married Life in Munich

Pitching woo—instead of a tent

As every GI knows, the thing that makes them most home sick is not mamma's meatballs and spaghetti. Despite the taste of Army chow, it's the girlfriend back home. And we lived for the arrival of those perfumed envelopes that were sealed with the letters "SWAK," and a red lipstick impression that assured they were. I was no different, and sent the future missus the most flowery description of Army life and all the benefits of being a GI bride living in Germany.

They say that necessity is the mother of invention. And I was desperate for the lips that sealed those perfumed letters, along with girl to which they were attached. I know that whatever flair I have for the written word began with the letters I regularly wrote to her. That talent must have won her over, as Susan Fay agreed to marry me, which turned out to be the best thing that ever happened in my life.

There were, however, a few other obstacles to overcome—like getting permission from the Battalion Commander and the local Chaplain, as well as approval for government housing and living off post. None of this was to come easy to a PFC. Compounding the difficulties, Sue's mother didn't think much of me, and was opposed to the marriage. Sue's dad had died of cancer when Sue was a young girl, and I couldn't really blame her mother for not wanting to lose her oldest daughter, particularly to a lowly soldier who would take her away from home and overseas.

After somehow gaining the Army's clearances to marry and live off-base, I was given a 30-day leave and flew home (I think on an airplane) to a big family reception. Sue and I were married on July 23, 1966. The wedding reception was modest. In those days it was called a "beer hall" wedding" and was held at the Throgs Neck Veteran's Memorial Post in the Bronx, New York. My Uncle John, a WWII Navy veteran, made the arrangements. Since neither Sue nor I had much money, I drove a cab for a private company most of my leave for extra money, and recall reading *Gone with the Wind*, when not on a run.*

My most vivid memory during the lead up to the wedding was a verbal free-for-all between our mothers. Sue's mom was so opposed to the marriage that she began pleading with relatives to talk Sue out of marrying someone who would turn out to be "a no-good bum."

While this was going on, my mom, a very feisty Italian mother of nine, began to answer in kind. While some mothers believe that the woman their son has chosen to marry is not worthy of him, Italian mothers believe that no woman ever born is worthy of mamma's *caro piccolo ragazzo bambino* (dear little baby boy). The result: two mothers, each of whom thinking the other's child not worthy of their own.

The feud escalated into nasty phone exchanges, which culminated with my mother threatening to break every window in Sue's mother's house. It got so bad that the priest who was to marry us thought it best if we called off the wedding

---

* Like all great novels, even though the book was over 1,000 pages, I didn't want it to end, which I guess is why so many wanted Margaret Mitchell to write a sequel, which she never did. Amazing how great authors can bring characters to life. I'm particularly moved by biographies of great American historical figures like Lincoln, Washington, Grant, Hamilton, John Adams, etc. who come to life in the pens of great authors like Chernow, McCullough, Isaacson and others. I don't want the books to end, as these men remain alive to me, as long as their words and thoughts continue on the pages.

entirely. Thankfully, after completing the obligatory "Pre-Cana"* marriage counseling seminar in midtown Manhattan, we were cleared to get married.

I had a premonition that the bad blood between our mothers would spill over at the reception and told Sue to be prepared to make a fast exit, if things turned ugly—which they did, but thankfully after we cut the cake, collected the envelopes and, paid the bill.

While Italian mothers usually cry at weddings, my mother had a few too many and got into an argument with one of our cousins over who-knows-what. When a piece of wedding cake went sailing across the table, I knew it was time to head for Atlantic City, where we planned on spending our honeymoon. We drove over to my mother's house in a car one of my sister's had lent us, to change and pick up our luggage. You might think I'm making this up, but the Damon Runyon inspired wedding we were enjoying got even wackier.

I had packed my few civilian clothes in a borrowed suitcase, but somehow managed to pick up one that my brother-in-law Tony had left in the finished basement where I was staying. Tony's suitcase contained his dirty laundry, which he'd come to have washed in an adjacent laundry room. I think he'd used a suitcase in lieu of a laundry bag, as he didn't want anyone to know that his washer was broken, particularly since he repaired them for a living.

Luckily, I found out about the mistake before we got too far, when I asked Sue to get a handkerchief. I realized something was amiss when she handed me a smelly T-shirt. But as they say, nature always finds a way, so instead of spending

---

* Pre-Cana derives its name from a wedding feast Jesus and his mother Mary attended in the town of Cana in Galilee (John 21-12) and was a mandatory course for couples preparing to marry in the Catholic Church.

our wedding night in a romantic setting, we spent it in a cheesy motel overlooking a parking lot on Boston Post Road, in the Bronx. And to be blunt about it, the occasion didn't need a fancy setting and the motel could have just as easily been the *Hotel de Paris* in Monte-Carlo—or a pup tent, as far as I was concerned.

The next morning, we dropped off Tony's dirty laundry, picked up my clothes and drove off to Atlantic City (which we would later return to many times for our anniversaries). I recall that the few days we there were heavily overcast, which, while presenting no hardship for me, was upsetting to Sue. She insisted we go swimming and walk the world-famous Boardwalk, and I dutifully followed. While the weather was cool and overcast, I managed to get sunburned and was unable to sleep on my back for a few days. Thankfully, Sue used suntan lotion.

I'd be remiss if I didn't admit that Sue's mother wasn't far off with her concern for her daughter's future. When I first met Sue, I was an under-employed construction worker who had dropped out of high school to follow his older brothers as carpenters. They say that behind every successful man there's a woman and, in my case, that epithet was never truer. I've also heard it said that "class" is an attribute that is difficult to describe, but easy to recognize and, using an old cliché, if you looked up it's meaning in a dictionary, you'd find a picture of her. Anyway, if I had anything going for me back then, it was the good sense to know a good thing when I saw it—and the desire to be worthy of her love became my life's ambition. It still motivates me.

The month's leave seemed liked it was over, almost as soon as it had begun, and I was on a return flight before I knew it. I was assigned "Government Quarters" shortly after getting back to the unit, and the three-bedroom apartment we were given was fantastic. The Army had rented a large housing complex called Ramersdorf from the German government. The walk-up had everything a couple would need, except food and toilet paper. A commercial rental in Munich at the time for a similar apartment would have been well above the means of an enlisted man.

In a stroke of good fortune, I was promoted to Specialist 4 a month after Sue arrived. The promotion followed my winning a few "Soldier and Driver of the Month" awards and the "Winged Tire" trophy from the 24th Divisions driver "rodeo" competition as well.

Sue joined me in mid-August, and I bought a 1956 Volkswagen. One necessary aside here: Germans pronounce the letter "W" the way we pronounce the letter "V" and pronounce the letter "V" the way we pronounce the letter "F" (as in Fowl). Thus, Volkswagen is pronounced "folks-vähgen."

Talk about "no frills," my VW had no dashboard instruments except for a speedometer, which displayed kilometers per hour, not miles. It also had an AM radio, but no fuel gage. It had a four-speed floor stick manual transmission and a rear mounted air-cooled 25 HP engine (About the size of a large lawn mower).

A small gas tank was located under the front hood—which had to be raised to fill it. The gas gage was a wooden ruler marked in liters (4 liters equal about 1 gallon), used to stick the tank. The VW got about 40 miles to the gallon, an important economy, as gasoline in Germany cost as much per liter as we paid for a gallon. Also, if you ran out of gas, there was a small lever under the dashboard which, when flipped, would give access to an emergency gallon, more than enough to get you to a gas station.

I loved my little "bug's" simple design and ease of access for repairs. So easy, in fact, that I was able to undo some bolts and disconnect a few parts and lift the air-cooled engine out by myself, when it died of old age. One of my Army buddies was an auto mechanic and picked up a little side money working part-time for a local *autowerkstatt*, so I was able to buy a rebuilt engine cheap and was even loaned the tools for the replacement job.

If you were lucky enough to own an early model *Käfer* (the German's pet name for the VW, which translated as "Beetle"), you would appreciate the love affair I had with mine. Since it had no frame (the body was molded flat plate), it could practically float. It was like the little train engine that could. I wasn't even mad when I discovered it couldn't make it up a steep hill with my wife in the car. She'd have to walk up the hill while I went back a piece to pick up enough speed to make it to the top.

The battery, which was under the rear bench seat, was always going dead, but the car was so light, I could jump start it on flat ground by myself. I'd simply push it as fast as I could, jump in and pop the clutch. Weighing only 1,600 pounds (half the weight of a normal compact car), it was like a kid's scooter with seats. And, since I never knew when the battery was going to die, I always tried to park on a hill, as I could jump start it by letting it roll a bit.

The car had only one serious defect, which is that it was only designed for a top speed of 60 MPH (when new). Worse still, the one I was driving had trouble maintaining the Autobahn's minimum speed of 60 KM (roughly 40 MPH), going up even moderate hills. This was dangerous, as most cars whizzed by at more than double that speed. However, the new (rebuilt) engine I installed had enough horsepower to easily maintain a minimum Autobahn speed, which allowed Sue and me to travel throughout Bavaria. The scenery was truly remarkable, and the little towns that dotted the hillsides and valleys were postcard perfect. By the way, if you ever happen to visit Germany, don't get too close to something the GI's called the "honey wagon" if you're passing a field where crops were being fertilized.

To better enjoy the culture of this beautiful area, I decided to learn German. Aside from the almost fairytale quality of Munich and Southern Germany, I was surprised at how friendly and open the people were, and particularly at the soft, almost singsong, sound of their words. My early exposure to the German language had been limited almost exclusively to the old movie clips of the guttural speeches shouted by an Austrian housepainter named Adolphus Hitler and his ilk. I was initially shocked at how much softer the same words could sound when spoken by the regular *völker*.

I learned that the University of Maryland had an extension in Munich and, with their help, was shortly able to master some of the more common expressions, like *"Wo ist die Toilette?"* Which reminds me of my first venture into a *Toilette* in the München Bohnhoff (train Station). As I walked into this large white-tiled open space, I began looking for the urinals common in the States, but there were none. I immediately backtracked, thinking I must have entered the *Damen Zimmer* instead of the *Herren Zimmer*, but a man walked past me and entered, so I knew I had not made a mistake. I got my next surprise when I saw him begin to relieve himself on a wall. My bemusement ended when I saw a horizontal pipe begin to wash water on the wall where he had been relieving himself. At the base of the wall was a tile trough I hadn't noticed.

I suddenly realized that the genius that had produced a no-frills car, had employed the same simplicity of purpose to eliminate the need for urinals, and with it, the long lines that oftentimes accompany them in public places. This would also save bars I've occasioned from posting the "Please Don't Throw Cigarette Butts in our Urinals, And We Won't Piss in Your Ashtrays" signage. I'm afraid that the same health department that protects us from the scourge of children's lemonade stands would never permit such an unsanitary device.

I was also surprised to see a youngish woman enter the toilet with a cleaning cart and begin mopping the floor. And no one paid any attention to her as they came and went while she busied herself sectioning off areas with her cart and pail as she went about her work. I quickly learned that this nonchalance was commonplace, and the Germans were much more relaxed than Americans about their sexuality, at least prior to Woodstock anyway. In fact, it wasn't unusual to see a woman relieve herself on the side of a highway, with only an open car door for privacy. I also saw couples getting it on under a blanket at a public lake I'd frequented with buddies (before I got married, of course).

These outings were enlivened by a special drink we concocted called the "Hairy Buffalo." The ingredients consisted of all the alcoholic beverages each of us had brought along, which were poured into a large pot borrowed from the mess hall, along with as much chopped up fresh fruit as could be pilfered. There was no defined recipe for this brew and the taste would vary depending on the quantity of wine, whisky, gin, vodka, etc. that was added. And as the pot began to empty, it was refilled with whatever was left over from making the first batch. This was great as we didn't need ice or a cooler—and after a few cups the flavor wasn't half bad. The hangovers were tough though; it's hard to get any of the hair of the dog that bit you when it came from a buffalo.

Anyway, I was anxious to start showing off my budding grasp of German, and began to use it whenever I knew I could get away with the limited amount of words I could command, like asking someone, *"Was ist der Uhr?"* (What time is it?). But it seemed that all the Germans wanted to practice English, as before I'd gotten a few words out of my mouth, they'd interject, "please speak English," as it seemed they all wanted to practice their English on me, rather than the other way around.

I knew I was finally making some progress with my German accent when I got out nearly complete sentences before I was asked to speak English. But my bubble was burst, once and for all, following an event at a local restaurant. Sue and I had gone to a German gasthous for *"etwas essen"* (something to eat), when a pretty blond, blue-eyed girl with braided hair and wearing the traditional German outfit came to the table. Before she could say a word, I hit her in machine gun fashion and my best German accent *"Gutten abent"* (Good evening), *"Bitte – Ich habe hunger– Ich will zwei Bier und schnitzel mit brot,* sehr schnell* (please – I'm hungry and would like two beers, and Weiner Schnitzel with bread).

The smile of self-assurance left my face when she replied, "I'm sorry, I don't speak German, let me get another waiter" I replied, "don't bother, I'm an American too." I could tell right away that she was one of many American dependents who we called "Army brats," working after school. Priscilla Presley was one of them. In fact, there were so many dependents living in Germany that the Army maintained schools for them from kindergarten through high school, as well as hospitals, shopping centers (PX's), gas stations, movie theaters and houses of worship for the service members and their families. And there were several colleges Americans could attend as well.

Incidentally, if you're wondering how a Spec-4 could afford to eat out in Munich, the exchange rate at the time was about four Marks to a dollar, and two meals cost about $3.00 — proving that two people could live as cheaply as one,

---

* Another thing I admired about the Germans is that bread and water were not automatically put on the table when you ordered a meal. Bread had to be asked for, and you were charged based on what you ate. Untouched pieces weren't discarded; they were simply added to full the basket for the next customers.

even before the "all you can eat" salad bar.

Living off post took on many of the aspects of a regular 9 to 5 civilian job, except that the hours were 6:30 AM to 4:30 PM weekdays and 6:30 AM to noon on Saturdays. The other part that wasn't quite civilian-like was the twice yearly, nearly month-long training exercises, as well as the sudden combat readiness drills, called "alerts," which were usually called somewhere between mid-night and reveille. Once an alert was called, all the units involved were required to muster their men and equipment within an hour, and to move out to what we called the "boon docks" or "boonies," which were local forests.

While I loved having Sue with me, she had to get accustomed to Army life quickly, since I had to leave her about a month after her arrival for the annual Oktoberfest-timed training exercise at Grafenwoehr. This was especially tough on her as she hadn't had time to make any friends, and we didn't have a TV. Her only outlets were writing letters, reading, and listening to the Armed Forces Radio. Our love of country music, which was frequently played, started there—and we always looked for local places that catered to the country music crowd after my discharge. While the local ones are long since gone, I can still wear my cowboy boots and hat at dude ranches that still flourish in upstate New York.

Looking back, I cringe at the thought of how lonely Sue must have felt, living alone in a foreign country. But that was to change over time, and she eventually loved Germany so much she wanted us to live there when I was discharged. This wasn't possible for many reasons, including the difficulty of finding work that would pay enough to support us, and the children that started to come the following year. Also, we'd have to get accustomed to a different lifestyle, as the German's weren't big on central heating and air conditioning. And apartments in the low rent market had shared toilets, with coin operated hot water heaters. In addition, the rooms were much smaller than what we were accustomed to, and the kitchens had small appliances.

Also, while the American military was welcome because of the closeness of the Russian "Bear" to their doorstep, I was wise enough to realize that a civilian American looking for work, might not be as well received. In fact, Germany, even back then, had many foreigners who had come to find work there. We became friends with one of them, an Italian who was working in Munich. Mario visited us often as I'm sure he felt a kinship with other foreigners. And it didn't hurt that I was half Italian and knew *poco parole* (a few words).

Happily, Mario let me try my German on him, but since he didn't know much English, we communicated in a combination of Italian, German and English. Unfortunately, to this day, if I want to say something in either German or Italian, I have no control over which language comes to me first. For example, before I get to *mi dispiace* ("I'm sorry" in Italian) — I have to get past the German *Es tut mir Leid* in my head. We must have looked like Mutt and Jeff* to anyone within earshot in restaurants, as he translated the menu and things waitresses and others said to us in a series of exchanges using three different languages that would have baffled any foreign agent not afflicted by the same malady.

Come to think of it, we could have worked for Army intelligence, in the same capacity as the Native American Code talkers of World War II, made famous in the 2008 movie *Windtalkers*. But teaching this language would have been difficult. We didn't know which words would come out during a

---

* *Mutt and Jeff* was the first American Newspaper comic strip published as a series of panels. The pair have become synonymous with any two individuals of different heights, which fit Mario at 5'-4" and my 5'-10" description to a tee, *sans* the horse racing and Ralph Cramden routines.

discussion, so how could we possibly teach others? In any event, Germany was a wealth of great experiences. And the greatest one of all was about to come to town . . .

CHAPTER 9
– The *Oktoberfest* and *Fasching*

Germany's answer to St. Patrick's Day and *Mardi Gras* . . .

Our stay in Germany was enriched by the annual "Fest" (feast) days that the country is renowned for, including the world-famous *Oktoberfest* and its lesser known sister, *Fasching*. The Oktoberfest started in 1810 as a celebration of the Bavarian King Ludwick's marriage to Princess Therese. Over time, the yearly commemoration became so popular that the brewers saw it as an opportunity to sell more beer (my guess), until it evolved into its present annual feast of food, music, merriment and, what else, beer.

The festival, held in Munich, capital of Bavaria, garners over 6 million visitors from all over the world each year. It actually starts in mid-to-late September and runs to early October. I wondered why it wasn't called the September/October Fest until the answer came to me one day as I was admiring the fact that some of my Nordic ancestors had discovered both Iceland and Greenland — and prudently named them to avoid their being overrun by tourists, as three-quarters of Greenland is covered in a permanent ice sheet, and Iceland is a Garden of Eden in comparison.

Applying the same logic, I concluded that the Germans didn't want any outsiders showing up to drink any of the special beers that were brewed for the event, until the locals had their fill. And it took a lot to get to that point, as the total amount of beer consumed during the three weeks of the fest was about 8 million liters (about two million gallons), most of which was presumably drunk in September. Having had the good fortune of being stationed in Munich, I got to enjoy the opening of the fairgrounds (and beer) before they were overrun by tourists. I was one of the few GI's to do so, as will be explained shortly.

Not being familiar with the customs surrounding the fair, I wasn't aware that the beer served by the liter (about a quart) was brewed especially for the feast, and had twice the alcohol content of the normal German brew, which was already double what was legal in the good old USA. Anyhow, my one and only experience there was on an exceptionally hot day and I quickly downed two steins of the best beer I'd ever tasted, before my body told me that I'd just polished off the equivalent of two quarts of Pinot Grigio in about five minutes. In addition to venders selling beer everywhere there was plenty of the "oompah" band music the Germans are famous for, and festively decorative venues serving food to go along with the beer. There were a lot of carnival type attractions and rides, as well. Sue had to ride them without me, as my head was already on the Tilt-A-Whirl.

As noted above, I was very lucky to have attended even one Oktoberfest, as the Army purposely scheduled all its local units to month-long training exercises in Grafenwöhr, during the three weeks the fest was held. As it turned out, the Winged Tire God smiled on me, as I was assigned special duty that required me to return once a week to Munich to pick up mail during the Oktoberfest. Otherwise I would have missed it entirely. (There would be several other special duties I was lucky to be assigned to. Read on.)

The other annual feast I recall enjoyed in Munich was known as *Fasching*. Unlike the Oktoberfest it started out much more humbly. The story I heard was it began when the breweries cleaned their fermenting vats each January and would give the dregs to the poor. When the brewers realized that a lot of those who had lined up didn't look too downtrodden, they made sure they had enough beer available to sell to the revelers once the dregs ran out. Fasching began on January 7th —the day after *Dreikonigstag* (Three Kings Day) in honor of the visit of the Three Wise Men (—who apparently, instead of their usual gifts of gold, frankincense and myrrh, delivered malt, hops and barley to Germany.)

But I had gifts of my own coming . . .

CHAPTER 10

– Grafenwöhr Training Exercises –
September-October 1966

Changing gears without a clutch

Our unit was in Grafenwöhr from early September to early October in 1966. Happily, our artillery did most of its live fire drills from the same position (they were assigned different targets), so our section got to practice running traverse surveys away from the base camp. And, luckily for me, my services weren't needed, so the unit chose me to make the mail run, which meant I got to drive back to Munich every week. That was great, as I got to take a bath and sleep in a real bed once a week. I also got to go to the Oktoberfest, as noted above. Moreover, I had time to study for the upcoming survey proficiency test, which allowed me to practically max it that October. This resulted in my MOS being reclassified, and the addition of proficiency pay went along with the new rating.

Aside from enjoying an Oktoberfest, there was another memorable event I participated in that involved beer. But before I get to the "prost" story, I am compelled to speak about some of the details regarding the reason why the unit went to Graf each fall (besides avoiding causing irreparable harm to German and American relations). Graf was a perfect location for the Army units to train for actual combat, in aptly named maneuvers called "war games," which, unlike many oxymorons I observed, made perfect sense. What else would you call an exercise where no one is killed or captured, and no one is permitted to fire their rifles except with blanks?

Our being away from the unit running surveys had another advantage—we were not required to immediately cover our vehicles with camouflage nets, prepare defensive positions and put out sentries to watch for the enemy every time we stopped. So, while we were enjoying the weather, the rest of the unit had to put up with being harassed by "aggressors," who were only distinguishable from our men by the white band worn around their helmets. It was my observation that that these "aggressors" could be readily defeated with white handkerchiefs, of our own. But that would not be very sporting. Anyway the "aggressors" played their parts with great enthusiasm, no doubt to return the favor of being harassed themselves when the shoe, or boot in this case, was on the other foot.

These mock engagements were overseen by white-banded officers from the aggressor units, who would judge the life and death struggles. And while it was hard to look at these exercises as more than just a pain in the ass, the outcome of the "games" could have serious repercussions, as I was later to see first-hand.

One night after returning to the unit, I was assigned to perimeter sentry duty. I took this role seriously, as I didn't want the embarrassment of being killed or captured and remained alert the entire four-hour shift. I'm not going to digress too far here about the fear of embarrassment being stronger than the fear of death, except to note that I read that the most compelling reason that drove both Union and Confederate forces to march in formation into withering musket and cannon fire, was the fear of appearing cowardly to the hometown boys who made up their units.

Anyway, late that night I began to hear rustling in the bushes, and knew it had to be one of the white bandana crew trying to infiltrate our lines. Thinking I'd turn the tables on him, I tied a white handkerchief around my helmet (*just kidding*). Actually, I remained absolutely still, which was hard to do, since, with all the noise this moron was making, I had to restrain a strong desire to burst out laughing. I soon realized why, since it wasn't one, but two morons who broke the first rule of an infiltrating force, *i.e.,* "Thou shalt not count thy chickens out loud." They did this by assessing how much damage they would inflict on the unit, in what they assumed was a very quiet exchange.

Their audacity got my dander up and, as soon as they were close enough, I gave out my best imitation of a bull elephant in heat and used an equally passable roll block learned on the playing fields of the good old Bronx Sandlot Football League, which knocked both of them on their posteriors. This startled them to such a degree that they offered no resistance, as I roughly grabbed and shoved them into our camp, white bandanas, unfired blanks and all.

Not wanting to lose the momentum of the moment, I continued to shove them ahead of me right up to our headquarters area. After unburdening myself of these would-be assassins, I rushed back to my post with the pride of having captured two aggressors single-handed.

You'd think that after such a show of valor I'd have received some sort of commendation, but I never got even so much as a thank you, job well done. Looking back, I realize that these "prisoners" were of no strategic value, not even for a prisoner exchange, since captured GI's were simply sent back to their own units, white bandana in hand, where they were expected to remain as casualties of war. (*So much for risking my life for such an ungrateful bunch.*)

The one event that stands out clearly to me was a celebration, called "Unit Day," which was the 24th Division's birthday. The day started formally enough with a recitation of the glorious record of valor and unit citations the fighting 24th had acquired since its illustrious founding. Left out of the recitation was the fact that during the Korean War the division was overrun when 400,000 Chinese soldiers swarmed across the 38th parallel and routed the American Army and Marine units at the battle at the Chosen Reservoir.

Looking back at the shenanigans of the unit I was to be stationed in next, I can't help but think that future Unit Days should include the 24th's glorious record earned at the battle of the Munich Hofbräuhaus, which I'd rank up there with another of the Army's illustrious unit campaigns, namely the US Cavalry Troop stationed at Fort Courage, (immortalized by the popular 1960's TV show *F-Troop*... I will elucidate on the history of the *Battle of the Hofbräuhaus*, a bit later.)

Once we'd finished singing *Happy Birthday*, each section of the 35th Battalion squared off against another in different "sporting" events. The sections included Headquarters Battery, of which Survey was a part, Communications (Commo), Fire Direction & Control (FDC) and the Artillery Battery. While I don't remember most of the sports events, I do remember the one that we almost won; it was a chugalug beer contest, which pitted ten men from each section against a like number from the other sections. After breaking up the shouting and shoving match that took place among the volunteers (almost the entire 35th wanted the honor of representing their section), the sergeants in charge settled matters by choosing the participants using the same democratic way they always settled such arguments — by volunteering the volunteers. This made sense, given the first-hand experience the section chiefs had acquired in the event, and because they knew which of their men had been banned from the most beer halls.

The contest was judged by one of the young wet-behind-the-ears lieutenants. Picnic tables were arranged side by side and one of the beer kegs was tapped to fill ten large capacity plastic cups for each table. At the shout of the German word *trinken*, the first man in each line stepped smartly to the table, shouted "Prost!" and proceeded to drink the cupful of beer as fast as he could swallow. Anyone forgetting to toast the unit had to put down the cup and start all over again.

By the way, if you're ever tempted to slug down a pint or so of very cold and strong beer, you'll find that your body's involuntary reflexes will immediately constrict your throat, making it impossible to down the beer in one long gulp. But we had the answer. The first guy from our section must have been a sword swallower as a civilian, as he simply poured the entire cup down his throat as if he were pouring on the ground. I mean he slammed the empty cup down so fast that the second guy in our line almost finished his beer the same time the other sections were finishing their first – we practically lapped the field. No way anyone could possibly beat us!

Unfortunately, we got greedy and beat ourselves. Our error was a less-than-sporting effort to have our section's feat become part of the 24th's lore, as we snuck our *Wunderkind* in near the end of the line and were unceremoniously disqualified when someone realized that the odds of having two sword swallowers in the same section was too much to swallow. But it was a sight to behold, and I still remember it with the admiration I have for a triple-play I once saw. (They are rarer than no-hitters.)

Which reminds me of a scene from the movie version of *The Odd Couple,* wherein Walter Matthau's Oscar Madison misses witnessing Casey Stengel's Mets complete a triple play due to an "urgent" phone call from Jack Lemon's Felix Unger. Felix's urgency stemmed from a need to remind Oscar not to eat any hot dogs during the game, because Felix was making a "franks and beans casserole" for dinner. Like the commercial says, Matthau's response was "precious."

Nothing else comes to mind about that time period, except that Sue looked like Christmas and New Year's every time I got home—or maybe the 4th of July. And the fact that my time in the old 35th was fast coming to an end . . .

CHAPTER 11
– 24th Division NCO Academy
– November 1966-January 1967

Showing my stuff— and nearly getting kicked out on my ass

The events leading up to my being chosen to represent the 35th Battalion at the 24th Division's NCO Academy in November of 1966 included being promoted to Spec 4 in September of that year, which followed my receiving the Soldier of the Month and Rodeo Driver Awards, as well as the survey proficiency rating, as entered above. My mentor of sorts, Spec 5 Bridger, told me some of what to expect at the academy as he had a bet with our Survey Section's chief as to whether I'd get booted out. He was almost right—I was called before the commanding officer, after a fight with a fellow NCO trainee who had provoked the incident.

The Academy was run by really "stract" (Army pronunciation of the word "strict," I think) Drill Instructor types, and reminded me of those I'd encountered in basic training— as well as at Leadership Preparation School at Fort Sill. The Academy pushed us all day, starting with the limited amount of time for the three S's (shit, shower and shave) in the morning, followed by squaring away our bunks, wall and footlockers for daily inspections. All this before falling in for chow and the daily training program. Any minor infraction (like shoes not being shined to a mirror finish, or your spare socks not being rolled properly) brought demerits, which affected your final grade.

Wanting to get ahead of the curve, I spent our meager savings from the month prior to the start of the four-week course on a spare set of boots, new fatigues, skivvies, and other articles that went into our wall and footlockers. Once I assembled all these mirror-reflecting boots and shoes and carefully pressed and folded articles, I never disturbed them the entire time I was at the Academy. Instead, I lived out of laundry bags which contained my clean clothes. Rather than gaming the system, I looked upon it as the strategic planning necessary for a future leader of men, like taking advantage of the terrain, or exploiting your enemy's weaknesses.

So, while other less prepared soldiers were busy spit shinning the shoes they scuffed up during the day, I spent my time studying things like how to harass the troops (*just kidding*), fundamentals of leadership, radio communications, reading maps and using compasses (called orienting). And, while GPS has now all but eliminated the need for artillery survey, back in the 60's we still had to do it the old-fashioned way, which required a lot of radio communications among the survey team and other sections like Fire Direction Control. While civilian radio communications like those used for air traffic control are straightforward, the protocol for military communication is made more complicated by the need to prevent the enemy from causing havoc by intercepting our messages and giving false information.

The subject brings to mind a related story, which you will appreciate—if not immediately, than a bit later for sure. To minimize the possibility of radio communications being intercepted by anyone but the intended parties, radio transmissions employed prearranged radio frequencies and user call signs followed by the caller's identification. The Army always chose call signs that would be difficult for the enemy to pronounce, such as words the East Germans, who were our closest adversaries at the time, would find difficult to pronounce such as the words beginning with the letters "W" and "V."

To further make it difficult for the enemy to intercept our

"traffic," each section had its own radio frequency and its own call signs. These were employed for communications within that section, and different radio frequencies and call signs were used to identify the caller when communicating with a different section on that section's radio frequency. All of which were changed daily. For example, the chief of our survey in our section might be "Whistling Widow One" to identify himself on the survey net, but he had to use another call sign, like Victor Victoria 20, when communicating with another section, on its frequency. Once the parties had established their identities, the discussion could proceed. This was done to confuse the enemy as much as possible. As it turned out, the protocol confused one of our fearless leaders, who, as I will explain later, ended up calling himself.

Where am I, oh yes. . . I need to talk about the fight that almost cost Spec 5 Bridger his bet. It started innocently enough. We spent the first day at the Academy going over the training program and the protocol we were to follow. One point was driven home—all the trainees, regardless of their present rank, were to be addressed as "Cadet So-and-so," and we were all to treat each other as equals. Thus, a staff sergeant could not pull rank on a corporal during the four weeks we were at the Academy. This was nearly to prove my undoing, as I took it to heart. And, when a sergeant pushed ahead of me to shave one morning, I took exception. When the sergeant showed me the stripes on his sleeve, I told him where to shove them. This escalated into a pushing match and after he took a swing at me, I knocked him flat on his ass. I helped him up an apologized and let him go ahead of me and thought the incident had ended, but I was mistaken.

Later that day I was called to a hearing, as the rat bastard had reported me. I told my side of the story and said if the other guy had gotten the best of me, I wouldn't have reported him, even though he had provoked the fight and had thrown the first punch. The board may have thought that this tough kid from the Bronx had the makings of GI Joe, as, thank heaven, I was permitted to continue. Had I been kicked out, not only would Bridger have lost the bet, but I would have to face my wife who had been living on C-rations, since I would have spent all of our money on a fool's errand.

Amazingly, the fight apparently didn't even affect my final grade or class standing, as I later learned I was to be the "Second Honor Graduate" which carried with it a promotion to E-5. For those who may doubt my being awarded Soldier of the Month, Rodeo Driver and NCO Academy Honoree in the span of a few months, I'm including a photo of the best present a man could ever want to find under their Christmas Tree: my beautiful wife holding our puppy "Snooky" and the plaque I received when I graduated the NCO Academy. Also, set before her, are the long-lost relics of that time, the *Winged Tire* and *Soldier of the Month* trophies. When you look at the picture, you may understand why Spec 5 Bridger told me that he had to hold up our Battalion Commander Captain Jessup when he stumbled and almost fell staring at Sue while attempting to open the door of the staff car that was taking them to the graduation ceremonies.

I was promoted to E-5 the day after Christmas. While I was certainly glad to see the extra money in my paycheck, I quickly found out that I still had to pull KP and Guard Duty. I couldn't technically be promoted until I had six months in grade as a Spec 4—so I wasn't permitted to wear E-5 stripes either. But it still was a very merry Christmas. And, while feeling more than a bit ticked off to be stuck pulling KP and Guard Duty, I resigned myself to make the best of it.

And, in a way, it worked out for the best as, unbeknownst to me at the time, I was scheduled to be transferred to another unit—this because the Army wisely doesn't want a newly minted E-5, which I was to become, to give orders to his former roommates. One event stuck with me that happened as I was walking one of the last posts I had as a guard. The post required me to walk around the motor pool one very cold night in January 1967. As the snow was falling, I listened to Buddy Hackett on the Armed Forces Radio station on a small portable radio. His jokes warmed me up like a hot water bottle. I must tell you one of the stories he told, as it is truly funny...

> A divorced New Yorker owned a parrot that she couldn't get to talk, though she tried and tried. Repeats of "Polly want a cracker" and the usual baby talk went nowhere. But the voices of the many visitors who frequently knocked on her door — including friends, deliverymen and the like — caught the parrot's attention as did the woman's oft-repeated response "Who is it?"
>
> This finally sparked the parrot's interest, and it began to answer knocks on the door with the same "Who is it?" response. Excited that the parrot had finally found its voice, she again tried over and over to get the parrot to say something else, but to no avail. It would only respond with the words "Who is it?" when someone knocked on the door.
>
> One afternoon, while preparing food for a small party she planned for that evening, she clogged up the kitchen sink's drainpipe with vegetable peelings. And no matter how much she plunged the drain, it remained stopped up. Dreading the consequences to her carefully laid plans, she called a local plumber and told him it was an emergency and would pay double the going rate, if he could get to her apartment in less than half an hour, which he agreed to do. No sooner had she hung up when she realized she needed an ingredient for the dip she planned on making and decided to run down to the near-by deli to get it.
>
> Only a few minutes after she left, the plumber showed up and knocked on the door, bringing the

parrot's usual "Who is it?" response. The plumber answered. "It's the Plumber." When no further answer was forthcoming from within, the plumber knocked on the door again, bringing the same "Who is it?" response followed by his "It's the plumber, lady." When nothing further was heard from within, the plumber, now growing impatient, started banging on the door a bit louder, soliciting the parrot's "Who is it?" By this time the plumber was losing his patience and shouted, "It's the plumber, lady, you just called me." The silence from within was now too much for the plumber and he began to repeatedly bang on the door and shout "It's the plumber, It's the plumber, It's the plumber" in sync with the parrot's predictable response. The plumber now lost it altogether and began to scream and bang on the door, had a heart attack and dropped dead.

When the lady returned with the sour cream and found the dead plumber at her apartment door, she looked down in horror and uttered "Oh my God, who is it?" The parrot replied, "It's the plumber!"

... I was always up for a good laugh. But the jokes I heard on the radio would soon pale, compared to events in real life ...

CHAPTER 12

– 24th HHB 1st Bn 34th Artillery – Will Kaserne
– March 1967

Did anyone say – Animal House??

As mentioned above, on March 2, 1967, I received orders to transfer to the Headquarters Battery, 1st Battalion, 34th Artillery 24th Division. And instead of running surveys for 105 MM howitzers, I would now be running them for an Honest John missile Battalion. The unit was stationed just down the road from Henry Kaserne at Will Kaserne, but the change, as Frost once opined, "made all the difference."

For those who have not spent the last ten years preparing to be a *Jeopardy* contestant, the Honest John was one of the Army's first land-based missiles that could be fit with a nuclear warhead. The M31 Honest John was developed in the early 1950's. It was a solid-fuel rocket, with a range of about 12 miles—which was less than the range of the Army's 175 MM howitzer. While the missile didn't have an internal guidance system, it was highly mobile, as it was mounted and launched from a trailer towed by a truck. Because it could not be guided to its intended target, it was basically fired like an oversized artillery shell, using its aerodynamics and the wind and temperature as well as the distance and elevation of the target area to determine its trajectory.

The fact that a sudden change in the direction and strength of the wind could dramatically alter the flight of the unguided missile was succinctly expressed in the words of a poem written by Henry Wadsworth Longfellow: "I shot an arrow into the air, it fell to Earth, I know not where."* The Army had a

---

* From The Arrow and the Song, (H.W. Longfellow)

more pragmatic way of looking at this: Given the blast radius of the warhead, what's a few miles here or there mean but a bit more collateral damage?

Also puts me in mind of a scene from the movie *Braveheart*, in which Longshanks orders his archers to fire into the scrum of the battle. When reminded that this would hit as many of his own men as the Scots, he replied that he had plenty of reserves. (The reason for these side anecdotes will become apparent a bit later.)

I was again lucky with the timing of events in my career as a few of the older squad members in my new unit were close to their discharge date and didn't have time to put me through the usual initiation rituals. Instead, as the only credentialed E-5 to be left in the section, I was promoted to an acting Sergeant, given a thorough briefing on the men, equipment, and vehicles that were assigned to the section, as well as the keys to everything.

An odd thing that happened to me a few days after reporting was being appointed to the "Unit Fund Council." I'm still not sure what its function was, or what I was supposed to do. The only reason I could come up with was that, since I had no prior experience in handling funds, someone must have wanted someone who was less likely to know how to embezzle them. And any concerns I had about performing duties I knew nothing about were soon put to rest when I discovered my sole duty was to look over someone's shoulder while he looked over someone else's. I must have done an excellent job, as I was later appointed to other similar posts. But I digress...

The memories I collected during my tenure with the 34th, recorded in the next chapters, may seem far-fetched—but I assure you everything which is to follow occurred as written, notwithstanding the absence of four-letter words that accompanied most of them at the time.

As part of the familiarization process, I was shown around

the enlisted men's quarters and was introduced to the guys as we went along. One thing immediately struck me—even the squad rooms that had a half-dozen bunks were squared away (for mid-week), which was a bit surprising, since inspections of the barracks usually took place on Saturdays. I initially assumed it was because a unit that packed nuclear weapons was apt to be populated with "a cut-above" sorts.

Boy was I mistaken.

I was to quickly learn that I had left an outfit of, comparatively speaking, misfits—to one of, comparatively speaking, miscreants—as their neatness belied a devious intent. And the "cut-*above*" soldiers were closer to the "cut-*up*" type. It seemed that their neat and orderly appearance avoided having foot and wall lockers subjected to random inspections, as was normal for the enlisted quarters in my old unit.

As we went from room to room, I noticed some of the lockers were open and the guys sat around smoking and shooting the breeze. *Hofbräuhaus* beer steins were in plain sight. I guess the neatness of everything fooled the inspectors, who probably assumed that all must have been previously vetted by that higher authority, since no attempt had been made to hide all this.

A few words about the Hofbräuhaus.* The main hall is about 30 feet high and 100' long and could comfortably seat a few hundred drinkers on long wooden tables with continuous benches, which sat atop wood plank flooring. The side walls had separate tables with benches or wooden chairs with the letters HB carved in open letters in their backs. In the middle of the hall was a raised platform where an "oompah" band

---

* The Hofbräuhaus is one of the world's largest and certainly best-known beer halls, located in downtown Munich, not far from Glockenspiel tower, which was a very large clock with life-sized figures which moved around like a cuckoo clock, as it gonged the hour.

played traditional German drinking songs, such as *"Ein Prosit"* which would be sung by practically the entire crowd, as they locked arms and swayed side to side in unison. The one that brought the house down was the "Hofbräuhaus Song" *"Steht Ein Hofbräuhaus"* the only words I can recall are "In München Stat in Hofbräuhaus, Ein, Zwsei G'suffa" (the word, pronounced "zuffa," means "Take a big swig.")

Beer was served in one-liter steins, which were filled at very large oval shaped barrels on the sides of the hall. These barrels must have held at least 1,000 liters each. The beer steins were carried to the thirsty customers by blond, pig-tailed *frauleins* in traditional women's outfits. Amazingly, these girls could carry five or six steins in each hand! You could also order traditional German fare such as *bratwurst mit brot*. (Think fat white hot dogs and hard bread). The building was about five stories high and had a huge flag with the initials "HB" on its stucco façade. Because the GI's were known to get rowdy when they had too much to drink, the entrances were manned by MP's as well as some very big German bouncers, who were always ready for trouble.

I already knew a lot about the Hofbräuhaus, having frequented the beer hall when I was stationed in my old unit, but was surprised to see so many HB steins in the barracks. I asked how they were acquired, thinking the guys knew where they could be bought at a discount. The answer surprised me. It seemed that anyone who was able to "borrow" one from the beer hall got bragging rights among his peers. I asked how that was possible with MP's and bouncers on every door and was told "follow me," as I was led to one of the two-man NCO rooms. When the door was opened, I was bowled over by the sight of a small wooden table and two chairs with the HB carved in the back. The only words that came out of me were "How in the hell." Boy, the inspectors must have thought the vetting was done by the Division

Commander, to have passed this up every week.

Anyhow, as I marveled at these symbols of Falstaffian pleasure, I was told that they were able to extricate the beer steins and chairs by a diversionary maneuver that would have made Sun Tzu proud. A few GI's would do the usual thing that GI's are famous for doing after having a few too many. So, upon signal, a couple of volunteers would go off to a far corner and start a fight, making sure to make a lot of noise while overturning chairs and the like. This attracted the attention of everyone, including other GI's who shouted "Fight!" followed by lusty cheers as the MP's and bouncers ran to break it up. As soon as the entrance doors were clear, a group would run for them, as if fleeing in panic. In their midst were some clearly "frightened" GI's who had forgotten they were carrying beer mugs. A few must have been truly traumatized by the sight as they even forgot to put down the chairs, they had held up to protect themselves.

Since I lived off-base, I didn't have to concern myself with the initiation rites and, given the risk of being busted in rank, would not have pilfered a beer mug anyway. I quickly forgot the "getting to know you" tour a few days later when I was put in charge of the entire survey section. It seemed that I was now the E-5 in the section that had a proficiency rating and had graduated the NCO Academy. Since I was now in a leadership capacity, my shirt sleeves now contained three stripes instead of the specialist patch.

I was to also learn that HB triumphs had led to one squad trying to outdo another for the pride of having "borrowed" the greatest number of souvenirs from the Hofbräuhaus. However, the practice became more and more difficult as the MP's and German bouncers got wise to what was going on— and starting a fight would no longer cause all the door watchers to leave their posts. The answer to the problem of how to pull off a coup in the face of a more knowledgeable adversary was answered one night. We discovered the results of the mission when we fell out for reveille the next morning and witnessed a sight that will never be forgotten by anyone who was present.

As I came out of the barracks for reveille one morning, I witnessed a scene straight out of *Animal House*. The entire unit was jumping up and down, screaming and laughing hysterically like they'd lost their minds. What could have caused such pandemonium? The answer was hanging from the roof of the barracks for all to see. Some enterprising guys from our unit had figured out that the one thing that the HB security boys weren't watching, as it was too big to be "borrowed." It was none other than the very large Hofbräuhaus flag!

Since under ordinary circumstances our barracks could not be mistaken for the Hofbräuhaus, once the officers got one look at its easily recognizable symbol, we were made to return it, along with the unit's other spoils of war. Thus ended the 34th's most gallantly fought campaign of the 1960's which, hereinafter, I dub as the Fighting 34th's Battle of the Munich Hofbräuhaus. A great disappointment. But we were about to meet one even greater—the unbelievably forgettable Staff Sergeant Waters . . .

CHAPTER 13
– Grafenwöhr Field Trip – April 1967

Under Water

My second trip to "Graf" was great, as we stayed in barracks for the most part and only had to run a few surveys. After we'd brought control to the firing location, we'd be off to set up three or four observation posts (OP's) on the ridges overlooking the impact area. We set our instruments up to observe the detonation of the Honest John over the target area that was chosen. When the missile reached its objective, a dummy warhead would set off a smoke charge, which allowed each OP to take direction and elevation sighting. The plotting of the intersection of these readings would determine the location of the detonation. Since the amount of time from firing to the explosion was nearly instantaneous, we had to be alerted when the missile was to be launched. A member of our section would stay back and call us on the survey frequency to alert us to the countdown.

    This is probably a good time to introduce you to Staff Sergeant Waters, who was to join the survey section later in the year as its new Chief of Survey. Sgt. Waters proved to be the most ineffective and disgruntled "lifer" (20-year soldier) we would have the displeasure of knowing, and his leadership deserves special recognition. One example of his penetrating mind was his inability to use radio communication protocol as intended—which was necessary, as he chose to remain at the launch site to alert us to the imminent launch of the Honest John. Here's the problem—we were required to use our own radio frequency when communicating with each other, while battalion employed a different frequency. And as outlined earlier, when on the survey frequency we used *one* identifying call sign and when on the Battalion net we used *another*. Unfortunately, the concept was a bit confusing to Sgt. Waters and he developed a kind of stutter while he tried to remember who he was and who he was calling. In fact, he got so confused on one occasion that he began calling himself, using his call signs for *both* the Survey radio frequency *and* the one he used when on the Battalion net.

Since no one answered Sgt. Waters' initial call, he may have assumed that the connection wasn't good—he started stuttering and shouting louder and louder, which turned into serious anger and threats once he correctly assumed that someone must be hearing him. Not being able to restrain ourselves any longer, someone hit his mic's talk button and answered, "You're calling yourself, you stupid bastard."

You might ask why we didn't cut this old timer a little slack, which we would have, except for the fact that he was a nasty SOB, who went out of his way to try and make life miserable for us from day one. His opening speech to us made it clear that he thought his primary duty was to make sure we knew who the boss was, and he'd put anyone on report who forgot that fact. He'd even tried to sneak up on us to catch us in some infraction or other. Knowing his tendencies, whenever he was required to advise on a launch, as soon as he hit the mic we started looking for the fiery tail of the missile, since by the time he completed stuttering his way through the "Oscar Papa (phonetics for OP) one. . ." and so on, the smoke that discharged over the target would have dissipated.

One oddity I observed during our live-fire exercises: Once the Honest John was fired, the launch crew remained at the site instead of beating feet the hell out of there. The enemy could easily calculate the location from where the missile had been fired, using reverse telemetry. But instead of making it like their pants were on fire, the crew took to cover that had been dug earlier. Donning my deerstalker hat and employing my best imitation of the deductive power of its most famous wearer, I came to the conclusion that these poor bastards who fired the missile could easily be within the kill radius of the 20-kiloton warhead they were launching! Ergo my earlier reference to the loosed arrows.

One notable event occurred when one of the Honest Johns that were fired failed to set off the small charge that would tell us where the missile would have ostensibly exploded, which would be quickly followed by its plummet to the ground. Since Graf was within a few miles of the then communist controlled Czechoslovakian border, panic set in as to the possibility that the missile had overshot the impact area and had landed on the wrong side of the border! The result was that all training was halted in Graf and hundreds of US troops and soldiers from the NATO countries marched abreast through the impact area searching for the rocket carcass. Unfortunately, nothing was found except some unexploded ordinance. Since there was a large lake in the middle of the impact area, it was concluded that the missile must have fallen there. Either that or the Soviet Union was more interested in whatever secrets they might glean from the spent rocket than they were in using it as an excuse for an international incident.

After these events, and long before we had to contend with Sgt. Waters, we spent the remainder of our three weeks running traverse surveys. Since we were no longer involved in live training, we were also assigned roving patrol duty, evidenced by the white bandanas tied around our hats and shoulders. Not sure what we were supposed to watch for, but since this got us away from the unit, we didn't much care and took full advantage of the freedom by driving all over the place at breakneck speed. There's nothing better than barnstorming around in an open Jeep.

The best thing about that trip was that our survey section had an opportunity to bond. And the "I's" and "me's" gave way to "us" from then on. In fact, when I connected with one of my buddies some 40 years later, it was like we'd never been apart. Thinking on the fact that soldiers could connect like that having served together in peacetime, I can only imagine how close buddies got who served together in combat. The term "band of brothers" is much more than just a catchy phrase. Our favorite after-hours haunt while at Graf was the Enlisted Men's Club, where all the beer you could drink could be had for 25¢ a bottle.

We enjoyed playing slot machines and "foosball," a kind of football or hockey board game that involved knocking a small wooden ball into the opposing goal. The board had three rows of a diminishing number of wood figures facing each other, with the goal protected by a single man. You could play one against one or two against two. The more practiced members of our squad could put a spin on the wooden ball when it was struck on the side, which would cause it to curve.

One night we were having a great time when our pool of beer money ran out. As we were dejectedly leaving, I found a quarter in my pocket and stuck it in a slot machine that was close to the door. It was our lucky night, as the jackpot paid enough for the group to order another 20 beers! That trip was the most carefree our section was to have in Graf, but the fall trip was to prove much tougher, particularly for the battalion commander . . .

CHAPTER 14
–Will Kaserne –Summer Fun, May-August 1967

Dancing to *Bésame Mucho* and Article 15's

We returned to Will Kaserne in early May. As alluded to previously, in addition to being appointed to the "Unit Fund" committee, I was also appointed to the "Safety Team"—and for some unknown reason the "Emergency Decontamination Squad." Perhaps it was due to my habit of taking showers every night or maybe because I had gotten an "A" in a college elective course in life-guarding.

Camp life settled into an easy routine. I got to put in training requests that required the Survey Section to run surveys in the surrounding woods and towns dotting the landscape outside of Munich. The training agenda I turned in consisted of duplicate marked-up maps showing where we intended to go, and outlining the survey traverse route we planned to take. Since the survey had to start and finish with known coordinates and be within sight of a prominent location (like a church steeple, you'll recall) from which to determine direction, I typically showed the traverse as a loop that closed out on the starting point, usually near a small local town.

Once we were at the planned starting point we had to find what surveyors call a "monument"—typically a large stone marker embedded in the ground. The map indicated where the monument was located, along with its coordinates. The map would also give the coordinates of the steeple (or other tall edifice) that was within the line of sight of the monument. From this a sighting could be taken to determine direction. In order to verify that the church steeple was still where it was shown on the map, we had to drive into town for a visual confirmation. And what better location to determine this than the local "Gasthous" from which we could view the church while we stocked our larder with a case of "flippies," which were bottles of beer capped with a re-sealable porcelain stopper. And we had a special place to keep this precious cargo from getting shook-up when we drove around.

Back before the advent of GPS the Army had a large and clumsy device that could calculate coordinates by measuring the spin of the earth at a given location. It was basically an oversized gyroscope which was called "distance measuring equipment," or DME, if I recall. Unfortunately, it had to be calibrated in some fashion when it was set up, which we never could quite figure out. Since no one knew how to use it as a survey instrument, we found that the thickly padded box it was stored in made a perfect storage cooler for the flippies. And the fact that we were desensitizing this DME device in the back of the truck seemed to be a good trade-off.

I was also given various off-base duties over the next few months that may have had something to do with the winged tire I had captured at the Drivers Rodeo. I'm sure that being married and living off post had something to do with it as well. Initially, I was appointed as the "Assistant" Non-Combatant Evacuation Order Non-Commissioned Officer or NEONCO of Battalion Headquarters. Later I was put in charge of the unit's Headquarters, and finally appointed as the NEONCO of the entire battalion. My duties consisted of keeping an updated roster of the names and addresses of all the unit's wives and children, and preparing them for rapid evacuation should the need arise.

The preparation consisted of my going door to door, introducing myself and telling the families I talked to that when they received word to evacuate, and heard me holler over a bullhorn, they had better drop everything and get on the bus

I was driving immediately—or risk being left behind. I had specific route and time schedule to follow, and once I had rounded up the families I was to drive them to a pre-assigned location for transport to an air base.

In my new-found status I became friendly with a lot of the other NCO's in the outfit and began to enjoy the NCO club nightlife with my wife. Once word got around that I was an OK guy, I was welcomed into the career soldiers' inner circle. In retrospect, I think it might have had more to do with the fact that their families would be in my hands in an emergency than anything else.

As I was writing the above lines, I found myself holding my wife in my arms and quietly singing, as we danced to the strains of *Bésame Mucho* in the NCO club one night. It's funny how we can turn back the clock for a minute and recall moments which, at the time, didn't seem important, but somehow live on so closely to our hearts. I guess that is why my memories of the three years I spent in the Army are still so vivid even after 50 years. Happily, they all seem good, in retrospect. Reminds me of the final lines from a poem I wrote, entitled *The Best Things in Life* . . .

A quiet time to reminisce, in memory's cobwebbed halls
And of life's woes in retrospect, it's worth it all in all

One more notable event occurred while I was still in charge of the survey section. A private, Michael Carmelk, was transferred into my section with a few months left in his two-year sentence, as he called it. While Carmelk was clearly an intelligent guy, his distaste for the Army was amazing and he showed his disdain in unique ways. They defied description, but I'll do my best to do them justice. When he arrived, I was told by our battalion commander that Carmelk had been transferred to our unit as a last resort, since he was "this far" from being court-martialed and dishonorably discharged. I was told he had been busted from Spec 4 to PFC, and PFC to private, as a result of the three Article 15's he had received. These are administrative disciplinary actions just below a court-martial.

Carmelk told me he had received one Article 15—when he reported for pay in his underwear. (A word about Army pay, which is probably carried out the same way in other branches: We were paid once a month and typically on the last Saturday. On these days we usually had a standing inspection, and often a barracks inspection as well. We were then required to report for pay in our dress uniform and to salute the officer as we stepped forward, when our name was called.)

Since the entire unit was paid in this fashion the line was long and it took quite a bit of time for the process to be completed. Anyway, Carmelk was apparently fine until the last few minutes, when he claimed he suddenly became allergic to the wool the dress uniform it was made from and had to remove it, before he went into convulsions. It didn't help him much that everyone behind him cracked up, turning the Army's standard practice into a skit from *Saturday Night Live*.

Another Article 15 followed his being charged with attempting to burn down the barracks—when he held a candlelight séance attempting to contact someone or something. And, given his dislike of the Army, it could have been the ghost of Benedict Arnold—although I don't recall asking about that detail. For those who don't know much about our country's history— which appears to have been supplanted by more meaningful college courses such as the study of *The Effect of Gamma Rays on Man-in-the-Moon Marigolds*—Benedict Arnold was a disgruntled general in Washington's Army. He tried to give the British the plans for defenses of West Point but was foiled by an alert soldier who intercepted the message. Anyway, the key point here was that the Army had its own rituals, and they didn't include candlelight séances.

The final Article 15 had only recently been given. It was issued as the result of a barracks inspection of Carmelk's quarters, including his foot and wall lockers. The inspector failed to find a single item issued by the Army—only civilian underwear, clothing, shoes and personal articles were found. When asked what had happened to his Army uniforms and such, he replied he had no idea. The Army apparel had been there one minute and gone the next. Unfortunately, I was too busy laughing when Carmelk told me the details and forgot to ask him where he had hidden his uniforms and such.

Surprisingly, Carmelk and I hit it off reasonably well from the beginning; we were both from lower-middle class families who grew up not far from each other (the Bronx and New Jersey), and we both liked to read and play chess. Also, neither of us thought much of the combat fitness of a few of the NCO's that populated the 20-year man ranks.

Our seat-of-the-pants assessment of military capabilities of some of the NCO's reminds me of a great scene from the 1950's TV show *The Honeymooners*. Alice questioned the quality of some steam irons Ralph was about to purchase. He had assured her they would fly off the shelf. We had similar concerns about following some of the NCO's into combat. Having not been in combat ourselves, our assessment of the combat leadership of these fearless leaders was bolstered by Alice's classic response to Ralph's sarcastic demand that she tell *what she knew about steam irons*. Her reply: "Nothing—but I know a lot about junk."

The basis for our assessment of the combat readiness of few older NCO's who had not seen combat was twofold. Firstly, anyone who had been in combat proudly displayed the Combat Infantrymen's Badge on their uniform (it looked like a flintlock rifle), and its absence was conspicuous. And, using Alice's wise council, we were sure that these long-term, low ranking sergeants had chosen the Army as a career; as they would have been unfit to hold down any civilian job more demanding than a night watchman.

This reminds me of the time a re-enlistment officer came to me offering a great deal if I "re-upped," as it was called, meaning signing on for another three-year hitch. I said I'd think about it. He later asked me if I'd give the idea the serious thought it deserved. I was very polite in declining the invitation, even though the standard reply to the obvious self-serving sell job was, "Yes, I thought about it, laughed about it, and forgot about it."

I managed to keep Carmelk from getting into any more trouble by appealing to the fact that, while he disliked the Army, he didn't want to do anything that would cause grief to other GI's like himself, and particularly me. When I told him that I was being held responsible for his good behavior (which I was), he toed the line for almost the entire time he remained in our unit.

He almost blew it shortly before he was due to rotate back to the States, after he started filling in his "short-timer's" calendar. This was a drawing of a voluptuous, naked woman, whose body was drawn as a jig saw puzzle with each piece numbered from one to sixty. GI's would fill in each day as they counted down to number one, with the more suggestive parts receiving the lowest numbers. Short-timers would suddenly shout out the word "Short!" to announce to all that they were getting close to rotating back to the "world," *i.e.*, the United States.

Anyhow, I was to learn what happened as Carmelk was strolling back to the barracks one day. As he crossed the parade ground, he shouted the word "short," and was stopped by an officer. Making matters worse, the officer had noticed that the US Army tag was missing from above the left pocket of his fatigue shirt and the word "SHORT" had been substituted for his last name, above the right pocket. In addition, the shirt pocket's button-down flaps were gone, as were the flaps on his pants' back pockets. When I asked him what had happened to the flaps on his pockets, he replied that he finally understood the fuss about always keeping them buttoned, as a strong wind had torn them off.

Carmelk told me the officer who had chewed him out was a "full bird" Colonel (a rank just under General). He said the colonel had pulled out a pad and said, "What's your name, Private?" — to which Carmelk had replied "Sir, Private (so and so)" — I can't remember the name he told me he used, but it wasn't his. I was skeptical about this and asked him what would have happened, had the colonel asked him for identification? Carmelk replied, "You don't lie to a colonel – no one lies to a colonel — no one."

The final straw did actually occur shortly. Word came back to us that after he had returned to the States for separation, he took off his uniform and set in on fire — which resulted in his spending a week in the stockade. Thinking back on it, I wouldn't be surprised to learn that Carmelk went on to become a wealthy guy in the entertainment industry. But — Carmelk wasn't the only character in our outfit, and where his irreverence for discipline left off, my good friend Donald Rush took over. And believe it or not, Carmelk's antics were actually to be outdone . . .

CHAPTER 15
−Return to Grafenwöhr − September 1967

The stuff that legends are made of

The return trip to Graf was uneventful, but the exercise wasn't. The unit was engaged in a three-day combat readiness test and we were harassed by aggressors constantly. In fact, while driving on one of the main roads to a location where we were to run a survey, our entire section was killed by a roadside ambush. At least that was the verdict of the monitoring officer when he halted our vehicles. Wanting to make our demise as realistic as possible, private Carmelk prostrated himself with a handful of daises he yanked from the side of the road clutched to his chest. When I explained to the officer that we had to be allowed to run the survey, so the unit could fire the Honest John that evening or risk failing the exercise, he commuted the sentence to two dead and five flesh wounds, and allowed that the two dead could have replacements "parachuted in."

More about Sgt. Waters is warranted here. He had been transferred into our unit before we left for the all-important combat readiness test. The officer in charge of the survey section, Lt. Matthew Bennett, also from New Jersey, realized early on that Sgt. Waters didn't know diddly squat about surveying and, heeding our not too subtle plea, decided he needed a personal driver with the rank of Staff Sergeant. Thank goodness he did, as only God knows what damage Waters could have done if left to his own devices. In fact, to a man, we agreed that if we ever had to go into actual combat, the first thing we would do would be to allow Sgt. Waters to accidentally shoot himself in the foot—something he was quite adept at, anyway. While "fragging" was a serious offense, we believed that a Court Marshal would find the action justifiable if not warranting a commendation, based on the likelihood that Waters could have fulfilled the role of the nail that cost one of Shakespeare's horses a shoe.

Lt. Bennett was about my age and came to trust in my abilities, possibly because I was able to keep Private Carmelk out of the stockade, and knew my "shit" when it came to survey. After the first day of our exercises, Lt. Bennett shared something that had happened while Sgt. Waters was driving him around that should go down in military lore, and inspired this book's cover. Many of the unpaved back roads around Graf had deep ruts worn in them by vehicle traffic over the years, such that you could practically let them steer your vehicle. Lt. Bennett told me that earlier that day he had suddenly realized that Sgt. Waters was no longer steering the Jeep. In fact, he was no longer *in* the Jeep!

As soon as he had turned off the ignition, Lt. Bennett jumped out and ran back to where he saw Sgt. Waters lying on the side of the road. Helping him to his feet, he asked what had happened. Sgt. Waters responded, "When we went around the bend, I was afraid that the Jeep was going to turn over sideways, so I stuck my foot out to stop it, and fell out."

While this event might be tough for anyone to swallow, there were other examples of Sgt. Waters' nimble footwork. Particularly when he tried to sneak up on our section after we had bivouacked for the night. One occasion surpasses all the others. It was dusk and there were deep shadows everywhere. Old Waters might have caught us off-guard, but we could hear him stumbling and cursing a long way off. In fact, before he reached us, he tripped and fell flat on his face, and was still cleaning dirt, grass and twigs off it when he finally came into view. We pretended that we hadn't heard him coming, and came to attention when he entered our night camp.

This three-day readiness test was the toughest I'd experienced. We were constantly on the go and didn't get much sleep, and what little we had was fitful, as it rained off and on the entire time. At night, we were required to set up a defensive position and pitch our pup-tents. And, since each of us had only one half of the tent (by design), we had to team up with a buddy to make a complete one. If you didn't have a buddy or didn't like the smell of the feet of the one you had, you could use the tent half as a lean-to. To keep from getting wet while sleeping on the ground, we always tried to find a slightly raised area with a level section on the top. To erect a pup tent, we had to snap the two sections together, then insert the ridge poles and drive the stakes each partner carried. And once the tent was set up, we would lay down our rubber ponchos, blow up the air mattresses and squeeze them into the tent along with our sleeping bags and gear. If there was room, we could get into it as well.

All of this took a bit of practice and, while you could do a decent job during a sunny day, the rain made it impossible to set up the tents without everything getting soaking wet. The memory of these intimate contacts with mother nature, particularly the ones we had in the winter, resulted in an aversion for camping only rivaling that of my aversion to long lines and their civilian equivalents.

I'm getting ahead of things a bit, since before we could set up our sleeping "accommodations" we first had to establish a perimeter once we pulled into an area for the night. While this was being done, we were required to camouflage our vehicles and, technically, dig fox holes. Thankfully, because of all the rain we were excused from that chore.

One particular night stands out. When we stopped that night, no one was eager to start setting up tents in the dark and drizzle. Since we couldn't sleep in the vehicles, we got the bright idea of making a communal lean-to. We took the canvas off one of our ¾ ton trucks and strung it between some trees. That got us out of the light rain that had been falling, and we promptly wrapped ourselves up as best we could and quickly fell asleep on our ponchos and air mattresses.

While we did take turns standing guard, the overcast and rain made it impossible to see much beyond our hands in front of our face. This is the reason no one noticed that the truck canvas had started to sag in the middle, even though we had stretched it tight on a downward pitch, to shed the water. In a scene that would make Charlie Chaplin proud, once the canvas stopped shedding the rainwater, it reached what structural engineers refer to as the point of failure and collapsed all at once. A reader's imagination will paint a much more vivid picture of the resultant scene than any further entry on my part can equal, beyond my suggesting that it was a "rude awakening."

The rain continued the next day, but that evening we got a chance to join up with the rest of the unit, and looked forward to our first hot meal in days. When we got into the main camp, we went straight to the chow line, picked up the metal trays our meals were always served on. These trays were same type you have probably seen in school lunchrooms or prison movies. The trays had depressed sections to separate the items of food into the various food groups, such as what we served that night, *i.e.*, dry slop, in-between slop, wet slop, and soup.

Since it was still raining, we squatted in our ponchos and began to eat the now unifying food groups. After only a few mouthfuls, the camp was suddenly attacked by aggressors who threw canisters of live tear gas into our midst. We immediately dropped our trays, donned our gas masks and waited for the tear gas to dissipate. Unfortunately, the tear gas hugged the ground like a fog, and covered the trays of our food, which was still emitting signs of warmth. Cursing our bad luck, but mostly the morons who got too carried away with the aggressor act, we just crouched there watching our food go from wet slop to soup.

I guess that was the breaking point for Rush. He pulled off his gas mask, said "Fuck them," and began to eat his food—which was still showing the lingering effects of the tear gas. This feat immediately changed our depressed and angry mood into one of uncontrollable laughter. That took a certain kind of guy that you don't often meet in life. And he was to later to prove that this, "in your face" attitude was no fluke, when he saved our section's asses in an act that, if seen by the general public, would dethrone the best that Hollywood has ever committed to celluloid, or whatever medium they are using nowadays to dip into your wallet, or bank account—if you add pop-corn and a soda to the enjoyment.

Talking about movies, there are two stories I enjoy retelling too much to pass up. The first occurred when I decided to play hooky from high school one rainy day and went to a movie. I've forgotten what was playing, but I do recall entering an old fashioned 1,000-seat theater that had two side sections and a huge center one. The reason I remember it is because it was totally empty except for one other person, who was sitting on the second seat from the right section, about ten rows back from the front.

Seizing a once in a lifetime opportunity I walked down the aisle and stopped next to him and saw he had placed a hat on the aisle seat and said, "Excuse me, is this seat taken?"

My other claim to theater fame moment occurred a few years ago when a few of my "kids" and I went to see a movie in the local IMAX theater. While I can't quite recall what was playing, I do recall regretting having gone, as the sound level was deafening—even to my deaf ears. Anyway, I forgot to mute my cell phone which was set on max volume, and, as fate would have it, went off like a bomb during one of the movie's few quiet scenes, accompanied by the flashing light setting which lit up the darkened theater. A fire truck on its way to a 5-alarm blaze couldn't have garnered more attention from those seated nearby. One woman, seated directly in front of me, turned and gave me a look that could have pealed two layers of paint off a wall, as well as the underlying wallpaper. In a moment of inspiration, and perfect timing that comes to us rarely in life, I held my phone out to her and said, "Here, it's for you."

Sorry for the detour; back to our story. When the three days were finally done, we learned that the unit had failed the combat readiness test and, with that, our commanding officer, Lieutenant Colonel Ray W. Cougher, was unceremoniously relieved of command of our unit. In retrospect, I don't think losing an Honest John during our last trip to Graf helped much either. I personally thought the Army made too much of its war games, but since our Honest John Battalion apparently had more fire power than most of the combined armies stationed in Europe, it's obvious why we might have been held to a higher standard.

This might also explain why we always seemed to be under a spotlight when it came to unannounced inspections, and monthly alerts that sent us scrambling into the forests that dotted the landscape around Munich. We also suspected that we were under constant scrutiny by the army's Office of the Inspector General (IG). My buddy Rush was sure that one of the Headquarters' Sergeants that palled around with us had been inserted by the IG, as a spy. He was a friendly guy who drove a brand-new Mercedes convertible, which seemed to eliminate him from suspicion, as spies generally try to be as inconspicuous as possible. But I had a feeling that Rush had a sixth sense about things and didn't doubt him on this one.

Anyway, on September 28 Col. Cougher was replaced by

a fire-breathing dragon from division—a Col. Stricter, who looked and acted like the late "Stormin' Norman" Schwarzkopf of 1990 Gulf War fame. Col. Stricter was an imposing figure of 250 pounds and well over six feet tall. I don't recall ever seeing him without a partially smoked cigar clenched between his teeth. The unit was called together for an introduction to Col. Stricter who gave us the kind of "No bastard ever won a War..." speech that would have done Gen. Patton proud. Col. Stricter told us, in simple but properly curse-laced tones, that he was going to turn this forerunner of F-Troop into a mean team killing machine—or die trying.

He emphasized that he would personally kill every last one of us "sons of bitches," and himself last, to save the Army from having to hang him, if we ever failed another exercise. While my memory is rather foggy on the timing here, I recall we were to be given another shot at passing the readiness test. To prove how tight a ship he was determined to run, Stricter was everywhere, kicking ass and taking names.

He even jumped all over our standard communication protocol. When a unit dispersed into its various sections, each one would call the other for a radio check on the Battalion net. "Commo" would typically start the ball rolling with "This is Commo, radio check, FDC how do you read me, over—" and each section would reply, in turn, and then to each other. We weren't half done, when Col Stricter hit his mic and hollered "Shut the fuck up! I hear you assholes too loud and too often." Someone, unknown but to God, pressed his mike and answered, "I hear you same, out."

Luckily it stopped raining and the sun finally shone and so did we. I led one squad while a good friend, Sgt. Robert Merchant—who was the Honor Graduate at an earlier NCO Academy class—ran the other. "Merch" was the most squared-away enlisted soldier I ever met, and we hit it off because, while capable of cutting up, we took our jobs seriously when the chips were down. While I was assigned to run a traditional traverse survey Merch led the other, but instead of starting as we did, from a monument whose coordinates were known, his squad had to determine the starting coordinates the old-fashioned way, by using the sun. This process was the same that mariners have used for hundreds of years, with a sextant (whose name derives from the 60-degree arc that it was based on). The principal involved measuring the angle between the horizon and the sun, or a known celestial object, at a specific time.

While my squad almost blew our much easier assignment, we managed to find an error in our work, as time was running out. While some might ascribe what happened that day to "Lady Luck," I believe it was an act, albeit a lesser one, of the same "divine intervention" that had pulled me back from oblivion throughout my life. One occurred when I was five years old and my older brother came out of nowhere to save my life after I had literally gone down for the third time. Another occurred when I almost fell 11 stories to my death but was saved by a scaffold upright which miraculously found my back. The upright was a 4 x 4 beam that occurs at the ends of the eight-foot-long scaffold sections. If I'd missed that upright as I stumbled backward, you wouldn't be reading about it here.

The initial failure of our survey to close ultimately resulted from the route I had laid out. It involved taping distances down a long slope—requiring the team to break tape frequently in order to keep it level (think of the bottom leg of a right triangle and the slope as the hypotenuse) across an open area and up an equally steep slope on the other side.

The route was much shorter, compared to one we would have followed had we stuck to the main road. That would have required many more set ups, due to its numerous bends, as each station had to be in sight of the one behind as well as the one ahead of it. I could add that I'd chosen this route to avoid being killed by aggressors, but I don't recall being actually concerned about that possibility.

Anyway, when we finished running the survey it didn't close, and there wasn't time to rerun it. While contemplating my demise and the unit's along with it—and recalling a number of times in my life that I'd made something akin to an impossible last-second shot with my eyes closed—I said to the squad "If you had to pick out one leg from the dozen we ran, which one would you redo?" After the group griped, hemmed and hawed* the instrument operator, named Bayer, owned up that he never thought we had a chance and had gotten sloppy with some of the readings. The survey gods were smiling on us that day, as once Bayer reread the angles of the one leg he'd chosen, the survey closed! Since the other squad's survey had also closed, the unit passed this part and we could relax.

Or so we thought.

The next day, rather than allowing us to rest on our laurels, we were directed to go out and run an additional survey, "for practice." We did as we were ordered even though the day turned out to be a scorcher. Not wanting to return to the unit too early, we decided to run another survey by employing the tried and proven methodology which went by the military acronym "GO"—which stood for "Ghosting Out." Anyway, we drove down a side road that, judging from the grass growing in the ruts, hadn't been used for some time. About a quarter mile from the main road, it turned to a small clearing where it dead-ended into a scrum of "dead fall" tree trunks.

---

* While you might think the expression was named after a prospector named Clem Hem and his mule Hee Haw, it was popularized by Shakespeare, for the sounds made by someone clearing their throat, when forced to speak.

Now out of the sight of the main road, we parked our vehicles helter-skelter and, in lieu of covering them with camouflage nets, we simply threw some dead branches on.

Since we saw no need to set out a perimeter, instead of taking that precaution we stripped off our web belts and helmets, laid our weapons about haphazardly, and opened our shirts to cool off a bit. We found a bit of shade under some deadfall that had formed a bit of a circle, lit cigarettes and began to chew the fat. What happened next truly had the makings of legend. . . .

As we sat around congratulating ourselves for finally getting over on the over-the-top war game nonsense, a captain with the white bandana around his hat walked into our midst, seemingly out of nowhere. It appeared we had clearly failed to follow the first rule of a "GO" exercise, *i.e.*, we got caught. In a total panic, we ditched our butts and started grabbing whatever gear and weapons that were within easy reach. That is all but Rusty—who I soon realized hadn't jumped to his feet with the rest of us.

It was immediately obvious that the Captain was going to relish the moment, as he began to question each one of us, in turn, starting with our lowest ranking members.

The Captain first addressed Spec 4 Petty, with "What's your job, soldier?"

Petty stammered "I'm a taper, sir."

The Captain: "Oh, you mean like a soldier who measures dress sizes?"

Petty: "No sir, I measure the distances between range poles with a survey tape."

The Captain: "And do you carry a weapon, soldier?"

Petty: "Yes sir, I carry a 45; it's in my web belt in the truck, sir."

"Nice place for it." The Captain replied.

He continued in this vane as he went from one of us to the

next. And all the time I'm thinking, "This is the end of all of us and me first, since I was in charge. At the very least, I'm going to be busted and that would be the least of my troubles, as this could mean the entire unit could flunk their combat readiness test, again."

As I stood there contemplating my fate, I noticed that Rusty hadn't moved a muscle, other than to take a drag from his cigarette. And while all of us had scrambled to put on our helmets and grab some gear, he had just sat there in his undershirt, like he was alone and had nothing on his mind.

I was getting more and more ticked off that he was making things worse for us, when the Captain turned to me and said, "What's your job, soldier?"

I answered that I was the chief of survey and bluffed that we were just taking a scheduled break.

The Captain replied, "Aren't you part of the 34th retaking their combat readiness test, Sergeant?"

I answered, "Yes sir, but I-I . . ."

He ended my sentence, "Didn't think you'd get caught?"

I stammered ,"Yes sir—I mean no sir."

The Captain replied, "Well no wonder, you guys don't know your asses from a hole in the ground, your fearless leader here can't decide whether he's coming or going."

In my initial panic, I had grabbed a grenade launcher which was within easy reach and the Captain continued, "That's an odd weapon for the Chief of Survey to be carrying, isn't it? Why don't you tell me something about it. . .what's the maximum effective range of that weapon Sergeant?"

I guessed, "Sir, the M-14 grenade launcher has a maximum effective range of 500 yards, sir."

He answered, "Well, you'd be about right if that weapon you are holding was an M-14 (which was a rifle), but you happen to be holding an M79 Grenade Launcher which has an effective range of three-hundred and fifty meters. — Who the hell put you in charge of this group of misfits?"

While he was questioning us, the Captain kept glancing over at Rusty, who simply looked back at him. The Captain was obviously saving the best for last.

Finally turning his attention to Rush the Captain said, "And what in God's creation are you supposed to be, and please don't tell me a soldier."

And while we all stood at attention when the Captain questioned us, Rusty had continued to sit on the log in his T-shirt, cigarette in hand, looking more like a civilian than the "Ultimate Warrior" we had spent eight weeks learning to imitate.

Rusty's demeanor got the best of the Captain, who now shouted, "I said what the hell are *you* supposed to be?"

Rusty just looked up at the Captain and said four words that should echo down through the ages.

"I'm just Fucking Bad."

The Captain took a step back and put his hand to his face to restrain what appeared to be his breaking form. After regaining his composure, he said, "OK you bunch of fuck-ups, get the hell out of here, before I write you all up."

We didn't need to be told twice and were gone like a shot. And to this day, I never heard another word about it. As I look back, I think our mistake, aside from not posting a perimeter guard, was our departure from the main road down one that must have left a trail of freshly crushed grass and weeds, leaving a trail even a blind man could follow.

While there were many memorable events for me in the three years I served, I think the one that most inspired me to write this book was my buddy Rusty's courage "under fire." I always believed that event needed to be shared with posterity, as an example of the American soldier at his best. In fact, I honored my buddy's courageous act in a poem I wrote, entitled "Rusty's Just Fucking Bad." The final lines of which read:

And now when in a bind I find,
No edge in showing fear.
I just recall his stirring words,
And greet it with a sneer."

And now for Round Three — a busted knuckle, a split lip, and a baby . . .

CHAPTER 16
– Return to Will Kaserne October-December 1967

No time for Sergeants—or MP's, for that matter

Things returned pretty much to normal when we arrived back at garrison, except that my duties now included Sergeant of the Guard and Charge of Quarters (CQ). Unfortunately, I did have another boxing match when I made the rounds at another company stationed on our *kaserne*. After the 10 PM "lights out," everyone was supposed to be in their room. But one night I found a guy wandering around in the hallway, and told him to get to his room before I was forced to write him up. He told me to fuck-off and shoved me as he walked by. He also said that he'd kick my ass if I wasn't wearing the Sergeant of the Guard insignia on my sleeve.

I'm not sure what happened next, but we started exchanging punches. And I know I hit him harder and more often than he hit me as, after a minute, I stepped back asked him if he had enough. He backed off a step, but then came at me again. So I pummeled him some more until he finally said he had enough. He left and I thought no more about it, except I'd bruised a knuckle on his head, and my hand had swollen.

The next day I ran into him on the stairs and he said he wanted to continue our exchange and invited me to go downstairs, to do it. I showed him my hand and said I'd have to oblige him some other time. He said OK, and turned away, but suddenly spun around and the next thing I knew I was picking myself off the floor and beginning to chase him down the stairs. I found out quickly why he had invited me to go downstairs, as waiting for me was a group of his buddies with open switch blade knives in their hands. I said something like, "This is bullshit—your buddy started a fight with me last night and got the worst of it—and he just sucker-punched me and split my lip open, so we're even." I guess that satisfied these morons, as they turned and walked away.

Sometime later I ran into this piece of shit, and I asked him what he'd done to knock me down, as I hadn't seen a punch coming. He put the shaving kit he was carrying on the floor. He must have known a lot about sucker punches as he said when he turned away it was only to load up his elbow, which he then smashed into my face. He also said he was surprised that I'd sprung up so quickly, as he knocked out guys he'd done this to before. What a fucking creep; if I hadn't broken my hand, I would have been tempted to give him the same treatment he'd given me. I later came to the realization that he was the type that ended up in prison or dead at a young age and wasn't worth my time.

Too bad I hadn't considered this earlier, as it would have saved me from myself. I spent a few years in anger management therapy later in life and came to realize how inappropriate my earlier "shoot first and ask questions later" behavior had been, and how lucky I'd been to have avoided serious legal problems. I can highly recommend cognitive therapy for adults, as it helped me deal with the issues without trying to figure out when or how the train ran off the tracks.

I still have the scar where my lip was stitched up by an Army doctor. He had told me he'd have to report it, as a split lip and swollen knuckles were obvious signs of a fistfight. I told him I'd had a freak accident by slipping and hitting my face on the door of my VW, splitting my lip. And that I was so pissed at my clumsiness I'd punched the car in retaliation and had bruised my knuckles. While he clearly wasn't buying it, that's what he must have written in his report, as I heard no more about it.

I also started pulling Charge of Quarter (CQ) duty which put me on a roster of those assigned to watch our barracks at night. The tour started after evening mess and continued until I was relieved the next morning, typically by arrival of one of the NCO's who worked in the Orderly Room. The hardest part of the job was staying awake. At 10 PM the CQ was required to go around and shut off all the lights. I did this by first flipping the lights on and off in the sleeping quarters as I told the guys in each room that lights would be out in five minutes. After I'd finished the first walk-around, I retraced my steps and shut off any lights there were still on. I did the same thing in reverse order at 5:30 AM, but this time I'd turn the lights on and off a few times and yell that the fall out for reveille would be in half an hour.

My evening and morning rounds were sometimes greeted by a chorus or two of a hymn we all learned that went "Hymn – hymn – fuck him." On occasion, a few more expletives were thrown in for good measure. We all cursed so often that it became part of our normal vernacular. Unfortunately, the habit wasn't easy to break and after I was discharged, It was all I could do to keep from greeting people with a "How the fuck are yah" and "You bet your fucking ass" and the always popular "Fuck you and the horse you rode in on."

I think the constant use of profanity by enlisted men was one of the reasons that officers were forbidden from "fraternizing" with them. I can understand that, as officers were always supposed to be gentlemen, and everyone knows a gentleman never curses, except when smoking cigars. I guess the enemy was just as profane, as our officers were forbidden from fraternizing with them as well.

One of the responsibilities of the CQ was to notify the company's officers and high-ranking NCO's in the event an "alert" had been called by Division. I was also the keeper of the keys to the Arms Room. This is where all the weapons and ammunition were stored. If an alert were called, I also oversaw the weapons being handed out by the Arms Room NCO, *sans* the ammunition. I experienced an "alert" early one morning when I received a call from Division advising that one had been called. This initiated a strict protocol we were to follow, including calling a list of officers and NCO's. While there were quite a few men living off post, each person the CQ called would in turn call others, so the list of calls we had to make wasn't overly long.

As soon as I'd finished making the required calls, I ran down to where the NCO's were sleeping and turned on their lights as I shouted "Alert—drop your cocks and put on your sox." This was the code word that was only used with this group of NCO's. They, in turn, woke up the rest of the unit, as I then ran down and opened the arms room and waited for the NCO in charge to begin handing out the weapons. Once this was done, I waited for the officers to arrive and gave them a briefing on the time of the call, and what I had done to start the ball rolling.

As was typically the case with an alert, it was still dark when I went outside. A lot of the battalions' vehicles were already lined up and ready to go. Once the commanding officer gave the word, the unit moved out of the front gate and headed for the its assigned assembly area. Any stragglers got to ride there—in the back of a bouncing two-and-half-ton truck, which remained at the base. I joined my section when the unit pulled out. Happily, we weren't required to do the full camouflage routine, and after about an hour of cursing the Army the alert was terminated.

One further point while on the subject: I was assigned CQ on Christmas Eve 1967, and couldn't get excused, even though my wife had given birth to our first child only a few days before. And, while on the subject of unfortunate events that befall us all, I must enter one that could have made it into

Ripley's *Believe It or Not*. It started with my buying a 1954 black VW from a buddy who was rotating back to the states. While two years older than one I'd been driving, it was in much better running condition, than my 56 VW—which was on its last legs (or wheels in this case) even with the rebuilt engine. I've forgotten what happened to my original VW. I probably sold it for parts to the German repair shop that had helped me replace the engine.

Anyway, I was driving to our apartment with my then heavily pregnant wife one night during a heavy snowstorm that winter. I was pulled over by two MP's in a Jeep. I don't remember where we were coming from, but I recall it was late as there wasn't much traffic on the road. The MP's came up to my window and said one of my taillights was out. I explained, I'd just bought the car from a buddy and hadn't noticed it but would get it taken care of right away. As we were talking, one of the MP's shined his flashlight on the windshield and told me to get out of the car, which I naturally did. One MP sounded like he was from New York, the other spoke with an obvious southern accent. What happened next looked to me like an example of why some believe that there are southerners who are still fighting the Civil War—

The MP with the Southern accent (who I'm going to call "Moron" from here on out as that is what he was) told me to get over to a brick wall, spread my legs and put my hands high on the wall. I asked why and was told I was being arrested. I looked at this moron and said, incredulously, "For a broken taillight?" He said it was because the inspection sticker on the car was expired, and I had been driving an unsafe vehicle. I again tried to explain, as I was shoved towards the wall, that I'd only just bought the car and didn't notice it. And besides, why would that require my arrest? I was told to shut up and shoved against the wall and patted down for a weapon. My hands where then handcuffed behind my back, and as I was shoved towards the Jeep, I said to Sue, "Don't worry honey, just drive the car home and I'll see you later."

The moron who had handcuffed me said, "The car stays where it is."

Beginning to lose it, I yelled "Can't you see my wife is pregnant? I can't leave her here in a snowstorm!"

The moron answered that I should have thought of that before I started to drive an "unsafe" car. I now turned to the other MP and asked if my wife could ride in the Jeep with us to the MP station and the moron said no. Now losing it altogether, I started cursing out the moron and, looking at the other MP said something like, "Why the hell don't you do something to stop this moron?"

He said something like he'd like to, but was outranked. So I was pushed into the back of the Jeep and continued to curse out the moron all the way to the MP station.

When we got there, I started shouting for the Duty Officer. A Captain came out of a back room to see what the shouting was about. I proceeded to give him an earful and when I finished the Captain asked the other MP who was with us if what I was saying was true.

When he said it was, the Captain lost it himself and began yelling at the moron. He also told the other MP to take his staff car and drive my wife home. I was uncuffed and given a cup of coffee while the Captain chewed out the moron some more and apologized to me.

When the other MP returned, the duty Captain told that MP to take me back to my car so I could drive it home and admonished me to get the taillight and inspection taken care of post-haste. So, the story had a happy ending. But before I left, I told the moron that if I ever caught up with him when I was out of the Army, he was going to have trouble chewing his food for the rest of his redneck life.

On December 22, 1967 Susan Nordstrom, Jr. came into the

world at the Army Hospital in Munich Germany. Baby Suzy came about two months early and only weighed three pounds at birth. I'm sure that the incident described above had something to do with it. Because there weren't any neonatal intensive care facilities as there are today, Suzy was only given 50/50 chance at survival. So tenuous was her little life, that we had a priest administer last rites, or "Extreme Unction," as performed in the Catholic religion.

But little Suzy was a trooper, and somehow survived. She was in an incubator for almost a month before we were able to take her home. Since I had to leave for winter maneuvers at Graf in January, I was glad that Sue would now have a baby to keep her company. Because Suzy was born in Germany, she was issued both American and German birth certificates and could have chosen to become a German citizen at the age of 21. Little Suzy grew up to be just as beautiful as her mother and became a Registered Nurse, also just like her mother. The birth of our first child put the bad times in my rearview mirror and I had only one trip to Graf left. But it turned out to be the prequel to the movie *Frozen* . . .

CHAPTER 17
– Operation Frosty Balls – January 1968

A new Winter Olympic sport

We left for Graf on January 7, 1968 and returned in early February. We had to endure some brutally cold and windy days, and it seemed like it snowed constantly. If we thought camping out in the fall was bad, conditions now were much worse. We were constantly warned about frostbite and the fact that our face, hands, and toes were the most vulnerable. While the Army's winter gear was top notch, it was meant for survival and not for comfort. Everything was bulky and cumbersome and there was no way you could run a survey with the boxing glove mitts we were issued. And we had to be careful our exposed skin didn't stick to metal. Luckily, the snow was too deep to do much surveying.

When away from base camp, where we were most of the time, just taking a leak was a chore, as you had to get through woolen long johns, the buttoned fly on your fatigues and the heavy insulated coveralls which had straps running over our shoulders, making it impossible to drop them, unless we removed our lined "Parker Shell" first. The term "winter exercises," seems like an apt description of what was involved. I felt sorry for the less endowed guys as, in such cold weather it was extremely difficult to coax their relief valve out of hiding. And if the "coming out party" was not soon realized, the result might have included iced up pants, and potential frost bite in places that would be hard to explain.

I had a much worse problem when old number-two came calling with no outhouse in sight. You know the old saying, "when you gotta go. . ." Having only two options, I had to remove my Parker and drop my three layers of pants. Unfortunately, this left a pile of cloths around my ankles that was within the fallout area, if you get my drift (no pun intended). Sorry, but I must throw in a tribute to Mae West here. One of her more memorable sayings, besides "Why don't you come up and see me some time" and "Is that a gun in your pocket, or are you happy to see me" was "I once was snow white, but I drifted." Hope the asides were worth your time.

Anyway, I solved the problem by finding a low hanging tree branch that was strong enough to support my weight and holding on with one hand. I leaned back as far as I could, which enabled me to miss my clothing. And using a technique made famous by the Japanese Sumo wrestlers, I unburdened myself.

When I think of the athleticism involved, *i.e.*, holding toilet paper in one hand while holding on to a swinging tree branch with the other, I think that consideration should be given to making it into a new quasi-Sumo Winter Olympic event, albeit without the need for toilet paper. It could be called the "Scheisse-baum."* It might even become popular enough to inspire a song written to the tune of an old Christmas favorite, *O Tannen Baum*.

As I alluded to above, the good thing about the weather was that the snow was too deep to run surveys or allow us to sleep in pup tents. Instead, we were assigned to 12-man tents with kerosene heaters in the main camp area, for the entire month. But we were required to simulate a combat training exercise, and I felt sorry for the "Air Watch" grunts, who were required to stand up above the windshield as we drove.

One day I managed to find a snow-filled ditch when I pulled to the side of one of the roads. My 3/4-ton truck almost fell over on its side as I drove onto what I thought was the

---

* German for the old number-two and a tree.

shoulder of the road. Luckily, my truck had a winch on the front bumper, and my buddies' Jeep was able to pull me out.

Another thing I recall about the field trip was a report that an M60 tank had squished one-half of a VW, while driving through a small local town one night (the tank weighed in at over 50 tons). The driver's side of the VW had been crushed like a pancake, along with the driver. The article said the surviving passenger told the authorities that the VW driver decided he'd prove he had the right of way by driving directly at what he apparently thought was a much narrower Jeep.

Not sure how they could have separated the driver from his VW; maybe they didn't. Thankfully, this was to be my last trip to Graf, as I was due to be discharged before the unit was to make the next one, in the fall, just in time to miss the Oktoberfest, as usual.

As I'm writing this, I'm feeling a twinge of nostalgia. Funny how time can blur a picture's fringes, so all that s left in focus are the things we want to remember. My next recollection was the "summer of our discontent" . . .

CHAPTER 18

–Perlacher Forest Housing and Augsburg Germany
–Winter-Spring 1968

Typing with two fingers and a bum shoulder

Upon our return from Graf, we began hearing scuttlebutt* about the planned relocation of all the American Forces stationed in Munich to Augsburg, Germany. We later learned that this was being done in preparation for the Munich Summer Olympics, which were to be held in August and September of 1972. I'm sure the Germans didn't want a significant American military presence during an international event of that stature. I don't think the Army brass wanted to deal with the possibility, if not likelihood, of an embarrassing incident (which GI's were more than capable of creating, in front of a world-wide audience) either. You may recall the nightmare that was to occur at these Olympics, when eleven Israeli Olympic team members were taken hostage and later killed by the Palestinian terror group known as *"Black September."* The world was shocked and saddened that an effort to bring nations together in peace was so utterly shattered. Unfortunately, it was just the forerunner of the terrorist attacks that are now commonplace.

    I didn't realize it at the time, but later surmised that the process began when all the Army families living in the Ramersdorf housing quarters were required to move to the

---

* The word comes from the combination of the nautical terms "scuttle" (to sink a boat) and "butt" (the name of a cask that held drinking water. Because people gathered around a scuttlebutt, gossip and rumors are also known as scuttlebutt.)

housing in Perlacher Forest—which was further from our bases, but underutilized. Our new apartment was in the attic of a three-story apartment house and had, in addition to the kitchen, bath, and living room, six small bedrooms. It appeared that the apartment had been a maid's or servants' quarters at one time. Except for having to carry groceries and a baby carriage up and down four flights of stairs, the new quarters were fine.

Aside from the hassle of moving from one place to another, we had to "clear quarters," a procedure that occurred whenever anyone moved out of government-provided family living quarters for any reason. The process involved a "white glove" inspection of rooms, furniture, utensils, appliances, bedding, etc., as well as an inventory of everything in the apartment that wasn't built in. The inventory was done on a form that listed everything signed for when I'd moved in, including the number of knives, forks and spoons.

I think the inspectors, who were German nationals, relished the finding of dust or dirt in places no one thought of cleaning—like the tops of doors. The inspections were done this way because the housing was owned by the German Government and may have later served as housing for the Olympic competitors. Sue and I cleaned the place like it was an operating room, as we heard that many had failed the first and even second inspections. In fact, those who could afford it hired a cleaning crew—who invariably passed on the first take. I suspected the reason for this was that they were related to the inspectors.

We were happy with our new apartment, but I had to again clear quarters when my wife and baby left for the States. They departed on May 20, 1968, from Munich's Riem Airport. While I'd had to pay for the trip when my wife first joined me, the Army foot the bill to fly her and our baby back on a chartered plane to McGuire Air Force Base, in Hanover

Township, New Jersey. I can still hear the strains of our Army Band unit playing *Auf Weidersehen* as my wife and baby boarded the plane. There wasn't a dry eye in the crowd of the tough looking GI's as we waved goodbye. I was not to see my two Sue's again until my discharge at Ft. Dix, New Jersey on August 31. I could go all mushy here as I recall the loneliness of cleaning the apartment and thinking of the three months it would be before I was to see them again, but there's no reason to awaken those feelings any further.

I moved back to our barracks as soon as I cleared the apartment—and spent the next three months working in our Headquarters battery for the Executive Officer (XO), Major Case O. Miller. Since I was due to be separated from the service, someone decided that I could be best utilized by cataloging, updating and completing the unit's library of Field Manuals (FM's), of which there were hundreds. I still have a copy of the Army's *Survival Manual*, which details the hazards and skills necessary to stay alive in jungle, desert and cold weather environments.

The article that impressed me the most discussed dangerous animals and plants one might encounter—with the polar bear being the deadliest. Polar bears are relentless hunters and can swim in open water for miles. I read that their fur is such an effective insulator that it is invisible to an infra-red scan. You've probably also heard that their fur is not white, and their hair follicles transparent. The discussion on polar bears boiled down to the fact that if you weren't a good shot with a high-powered rifle when you encountered one, you were dead meat and would be eaten alive—if you failed to save the last bullet . . . for yourself.

I enjoyed this desk job. It required a lot of typing, which I later put to good use. I also enjoyed the flights I was authorized to take on a single-engine scout plane to Division Headquarters, in order to expedite the form work process. I was given a "Confidential" clearance for the job, which was quite a feat after having been arrested three times, twice for assault, before the age of 18. In my spare time I also did a lot of running, which was a lifelong joy of mine. I'd read James Fenimore Cooper's *The Dear Slayer* and *The Last of the Mohicans* as a young boy and was taken by the main character's ability to run all day. I typically clipped off five miles a night whenever I got a chance. (I could do ten miles without much trouble up to age 55, but wore my knees out and had to have partial knee replacements in my mid-60's.)

The best part of running for me was that when I found a place where my mind, breathing, body, and legs came into perfect sync I felt I could run effortlessly, forever. And a wonderful serenity came over me once I stopped, particularly when I sprinted the last 220 yards. That would produce a pleasant high—courtesy of the brain's released endorphins. Too bad they couldn't manufacture this natural high, as it would do what cannabis and other mind-altering chemicals do, without the side effects!

I must also relate an incident, or more appropriately, an *accident*, that occurred late in my enlistment, which at the time didn't mean much to me, but was to play a significant role in my later life. It happened one afternoon while the unit's younger NCO's played a pick-up game of softball against the young officers. I was catching, and there was a second lieutenant on second base when the batter hit a line drive to the outfield. The throw home got to me about the same time as the runner. As I squatted to take the throw, instead of sliding, the bastard came flying into my left shoulder feet first—and knocked me on my ass. Being young and tough, I just shook it off, as I did whenever I got hurt playing football. I recall the coach always telling us to "Walk it off." And that's what I did. I finished the game but was in a lot of pain. After the game I put hot towels on it for a few days and took Aspirin. Luckily for me, I went to see an Army doctor, who made a report of the "accident." Had they been able to do an MRI or CAT scan back then, the result would have shown a lot of damage. But the fact that the injury was in my record proved significant years later when I had surgery done on my shoulder. More importantly, I was then given a 20% disability rating by the Army, which qualified me to bid on government construction projects that are set aside for veterans like myself. When I landed my first VA contract, I stopped damning that second lieutenant, and began thanking him.

Moving on, in spite of all the negatives I was starting to see the light at the end of the tunnel . . .

CHAPTER 19
– "Short-timer" – June-August 1968

A Hallowed Army Tradition

As I counted them down, the last 60 days of my enlistment seemed like they would never end. I was lonely and a bit depressed having not seen my wife and baby for months. I grew even more melancholy upon learning Sue had gotten pregnant with our second child, shortly before leaving. But what's important at this point were the traditions that accompanied being "short," which officially started 60 days prior to being shipped home. I described a short-timer's calendar earlier—now I was filling in my own.

In addition to the calendar, there was a *short-timer*'s form letter that was sent home to alert the folks of what to expect when a soldier returns home. The letter listed some of the foreign words that might be used including "Nein" (pronounced like the number nine), meaning "no," and the ever popular, *"Mach Nicht"* (we pronounced it "Mox Nix"), a German slang expression meaning "makes no difference," or "no big deal." Our civilian friends might also be treated to the combined terms "nicht" and "nein," as follows (using the American vernacular): "Nix-Nine-Fuck no." The letter also suggested that the folks lock up all their beer, wine and liquor, and to warn the neighbors to hide their daughters, as GI Joe is coming back to the "world."

It was tough saying goodbye to my buddies, when it came time to leave. I knew I'd probably never see or talk to many of them again. Since most of them were from were from different states, I extended an invitation to stay with me when they got out, and I'd show them the sights of New York City. A few took me up on my offer. Funny, while a native New York, I'd taken some of the more well-known sites for granted and, it wasn't until I was showing my buddies around that I got to see Manhattan from the observation deck of the Empire State Building and World Trade Center towers.

Happily, I had gone to the major museums, zoos, etc., when I was younger, and was lucky enough to climb up the narrow spiral staircase of the Statue of Liberty's arm to her torch, before it was closed to tourists. Another sight I remember well was the Lowe's Paradise Theater on Fordham road — where I'd gone to see Rogers and Hammerstein's *South Pacific*, when I was 16. It's one of the last classic movie houses and worth the price of admission. In addition to the fantastic architectural details, the sky-colored vaulted ceiling contained tiny lighted stars outlining the major constellations, as clouds magically floating across the scene. Its unique features aside, there's a real reason I remember the theater and ceiling so well. I had gone thinking that "South Pacific" was a war movie and was disgusted by the constant singing and weird lighting effects to such an extent that another song would commence, I stared up at the ceiling as if praying for the war gods to intervene. And while I kept waiting for the war to begin, all I got for my trouble was another song. Life seems to be that way sometimes, doesn't it? While we're waiting for the action to begin, we only later realize that the real action was there all along. While I grew to love the movie over time, the bloom came off the rose for me when I learned that Mitzi Gaynor was the only cast member to use her own voice. Rossano Brazzi lost some of the "Enchantment" for me when I learned that Metropolitan Opera baritone Giorgio Tozzi was singing behind the curtain.

How did I get so far off track? Anyway, as part of the final pre-discharge process, I had to obtain sign-offs from different sections, including medical, supply, and whoever else was involved. Since I'd been assigned to a Major Miller, this was easy enough. As part of the medical clearance I had to take a final physical, which I cheated a bit on— if I'd said my shoulder was messed up, I was afraid I'd be kept on active duty.

While this was going on, I got the only real scare of my enlistment, as what became known as the "Czechoslovakian crisis" was growing more intense by the week. In fact, all of NATO's forces were placed on high alert. The situation started when a reformist by the name of Alexander Dubcek was elected as head of the Czech Communist Party and announced plans to grant more rights to the people by decentralizing the economy and democratization. The movement was crushed by Soviet Tanks the month I was due to be shipped home.

My fear wasn't as much connected to a potential war with the Soviet Union as it was with the thought of my service time being extended. For, while I was ready to spit in comrade Brezhnev's eye, I was sure NATO would sit on its hands, as democracies always do, until war is visited upon them. I'd grown up in a tough neighborhood and knew that the best way to avoid fights was to kick the shit out of the first person who came looking for one. After that, no one else wanted to fuck with you. But that's a topic for another time.

In late July I received orders to report to the Rheim/Main Air Base in Frankfurt. Just before leaving I sold my 1954 VW to one of my buddies and gave away some of the paraphernalia I'd accumulated over the course of my tour of duty— including Christmas decorations, transformers (to convert the German electric current for use with American devices), and the like. It was hard to believe my Army days were over!

Almost . . .

CHAPTER 20

−Mustering Out − The GI Bill − Sept 1968

Auf Weidersehen

In late July I received orders to report to the Rheim/Main Air Base in Frankfurt for transport back to CONUS (Continental United States). The flight was on August 30$^{th.}$ The plane landed at McGuire Air Force Base in New Jersey and I was bused back to where it all started almost three years earlier, for the processing of my discharge paperwork. My wife and her brother had driven two cars out to meet me when I arrived, since I wasn't sure how long it would take to complete the process and left one for me to drive home. The final paperwork took a few days and I was issued my final paycheck ("mustering out pay")— which included money for unused leave time.

I thought about my friend Carmelk, as I took off my uniform for the last time and officially became a civilian. I recall the drive home, as I'd given a lift back to New York to another GI, who told me some horseshit story about why he'd been kicked out of the service. I knew he was lying and figured he was just rehearsing what he wanted to tell his family and friends, to see how it would go over. I knew his story would not have fooled anyone, except maybe his mother, and feeling sorry for her, told him a story that was more outrageous than his, hoping he'd realize how fruitless it would be to tell a series of lies. When he accepted my story, I knew there was no hope for his mother.

Speaking of which—when I got back to my own mother and father's house in Pelham Bay, I found a big "Welcome Home" banner hanging off the side of the front doorsteps. A lot of family friends and even a few neighbors had turned out for my homecoming party.

It felt strange to be a civilian again, but with a wife, baby, and another on the way, I didn't have time to rest on my laurels, and started job hunting right away.

One of my good friends was at the party and showed me a 32-caliber pistol he intended to use for a down payment on a house. I begged him not to do whatever he had planned on doing, to no avail. Lucky for him, the law caught up with him after he'd made an unscheduled withdrawal from a bank on City Island in the Bronx—and after spending a time as a guest of New York State, he changed his life around. In a few years he made his way to California, where he became a successful contractor. I could add a few more stories of this type, but since this book was written about my time in the Army, I'll have to let them go for another day.

Luckily, I found work as a carpenter shortly after returning home. I had another streak of luck when I ran into an old friend who was working for a major New York construction management firm. He got me a job as an assistant field superintendent on a project in Greenwich, Connecticut. This led to being hauled into the company's main office in Manhattan when they discovered that I could read and write better than most of their assistant project managers—one of which I quickly became.

While working in New York, I enrolled in engineering courses at Bronx Community College and went there for four years of night school and earned an associate degree. I then transferred to the City College of New York (CCNY) to continue studies towards a degree in Civil Engineering, which I never quite managed to complete. After compiling a total of 93 credits, the last ones coming at CCNY, the stress of working full time while trying to raise a family (which now totaled four) became too much for me. When we moved to Rockland

County in 1978, I dropped out.

The good news was that I had been able to save up the monthly payments I received for tuition under the GI bill, since the New York University tuition was free. That extra money became the down payment on our first house. We later sold that house when we moved to the one I still own in Rockland County, NY—the home in which Sue and I raised our five children.

My Army days are long gone, but are somehow still with me. I now officially close this proudest chapter of my life with words borrowed from time-honored military tradition that have gained new meaning in the minds and hearts of the civilian population of our beloved country:

SNAFU —Situation Normal All Fucked Up

If you're still reading, thank you, and I hope you paid for your copy!

POSTSCRIPT

While this book was written as a comedic tale of garrison life in the Army of the mid-sixties, I look back on my service with pride and see it as the most eventful three years of my life. I also still feel a bit of a twinge of conscience for other Americans, including a few I knew as a young man, who had given their lives in the jungles of Viet Nam while I was enjoying life in a duty station free of the turmoil and death. While I've taken some pot shots at the Army in the foregoing, I am truly honored to have served and have a great deal of respect for the vast majority of men with whom I had the honor to serve. The Officers' Corp and virtually all the NCO's I served with were professional soldiers and stood between the careless civilian population of America and Europe and the forces that would destroy our freedoms, had they not feared the consequences of trying to do so.

I find it interesting that freedom-seeking peoples throughout the world, most recently in Hong Kong and Iran, can be seen waving American flags in the hope that we will come to their rescue. If you're interested in what I have to say about this, and many other topics, including why I believe The Paris Agreement (*aka* the Paris climate accord) was seriously flawed, stay tuned for my next book: *Off the Beaten Path*. This work is based on a compilation of podcast shows I hosted on *talkradionyc.com.*, including one which asked why the accord gave a free pass to China until the year 2030, as it was considered a "Developing Nation." That show further asked why the 2016 accord had failed to address the destruction of the rain forests in South America and the loss of coral reefs.

ABOUT THE AUTHOR

Situation Normal A. F. U. is Oscar R. Nordstrom's third book. In addition to writing books and poetry, Nordstrom is the recipient of numerous awards and testimonials for public service and charitable works. Born in March of 1944, one of nine children to second generation Swedish and Italian parents, he lived in housing projects in the Bronx, New York in his formative years. His mother, like many of her generation, had only a grammar school education, but she somehow found time amid the bedlam of raising nine children to consume the Reader's Digest condensed books that arrived monthly at their Bronx home. Her interest in the best sellers of that day instilled in Oscar a love of books and literature from an early age.

The premature death of his wife to esophageal cancer was a life-changing experience for Nordstrom, eventually leading to a personal renaissance that included learning to sail, delving into opera, traveling, acting, and developing a talent for poetry. While continuing to run his family contracting and consulting firm with his sons, Oscar turned his focus to writing.

His life-long love of books and poetry, art, history, world religions, and the sciences all contributed to the writing of his first book, the critically praised *Fountain of Change: How the Life and Ideas of Jesus Reshaped Our World*. Oscar's life experiences, education, and breadth of interests have given him a unique perspective on the life and ideas of world's most famous individual, Jesus of Nazareth, allowing him to show Jesus as a social reformer, philosopher, and teacher, absent the religious trappings that surround him. Nordstrom also published *Pleasant Surprises: Inspiring Rhymes for Special Times*, a compilation of his poetry and verse.

ARMY TERMS, ACRONYMS AND SLANG USED IN THIS BOOK

AWOL – Absent Without Leave
Barracks – Military housing
Bunk – Frame and spring bed
C-Rations – Combat Rations (meals in a box)
CO – Commanding Officer (Battalion, Division, etc.)
CONUS – Continental United States
CQ – Charge of Quarters (After-hour NCO in Charge)
DI – Drill Instructor (Training Instructor)
DME – Distance Measuring Equipment (Early GPS Device)
Dog Tags – Metal ID tag worn about the neck
Double Time – Jogging in formation
Duffle Bag – Large canvas bag (military luggage)
Fatigues – Daily clothing (pants, shirt, jacket and soft hat)
FDC – Fire Direction Control (Artillery section which directs fire)
FO – Forward Observer (reports enemy position)
FTA – Fun Travel Adventure; Finest Training Available
General Orders –

> To take charge of this post and all government property in view.
>
> To walk my post in a military manner, keeping always on the alert and observing everything that takes place within sight or hearing.
>
> To report all violations of orders I am instructed to enforce.
>
> To repeat all calls from any post to those more distant from my own.
>
> To quit my post only when properly relieved.
>
> To receive, obey, and pass on to the sentry who relieves me, all orders from the Sergeant of the Guard and Offi-

cers of the watch only.

To talk to no one except in the line of duty.

To give the alarm in case of fire or disorder.

To call the Sergeant of the Guard in any case not covered by instructions.

To salute all officers and all colors and standards not cased.

To be especially watchful at night and during the time for challenging, to challenge all persons on or near my post, and allow no one to pass without proper authority.

GI – General Issue (slang for any enlisted or drafted personal)

GP – General Purpose (genesis of the word "jeep)

Gun Bunny – Artillery soldier analogous to an infantryman grunt

HHB – Headquarters Battery

IG – Inspectors General (Authority charged with preventing waste, fraud, abuse and mismanagement in Army units)

jeep – M151 Army all-purpose 1/4-ton vehicle

KP – Kitchen Police (Potato peeling and mop brigade)

KM – Kilometer (Metric distance - approx. 1.6 miles)

Logbook – Record of vehicle usage and maintenance

Mess – Aptly named military term for meals and the place where served

MOS – Military Occupational Specialty (Cook, Mechanic, Surveyor, etc.)

MP – Military Police

NCO – Non-Commissioned Officer (Corporal or Sergeant)

NEONCO – Non-Combatant (Civilian) Evacuation Operation NCO

NG – National Guard

OCS – Officers' Candidate School (enlisted personal officer training)

OP – Observation Post (military radio jargon is Oscar Poppa)

Orderly Room – Unit's Administrative offices

PFC - Private First Class (military rank of E-3)

Pup Tent – Two-man tent (Each man carries one half.)

PX – Post Exchange (Army shopping center and department store)

RA – Regular Army (Prefix for Enlisted personal service number)

Roger – (radio jargon for "understood")

SFC – Sergeant First Class

Short – Short-timer (GI's last 60 days before shipping home)

Spec-4 – Specialist E-4 (non-command occupation *i.e.*, cook, etc.)

Spit-Shine – Shoe-shining practice using phlegm or water

US – United States (Prefix for drafted personal service number)

WILCO – Will Comply (radio jargon for "will obey request or command")

XO – Executive Officer (Second in command of a unit)

PHOTOS

Inoculations for new recruits.
October, 1965
Two shots for the price of one.
(See Page 41)

Rifle drill. Oscar at left.
October 1965
Port Arms isn't a waterfront hotel.
(See Page 43)

Rifle training, Ft. Dix
September, 1965
Stop closing both eyes and you might hit the target!
(See Page 44)

CBR training—tear gas.
November, 1965
Don't try this at home!
(See Page 46)

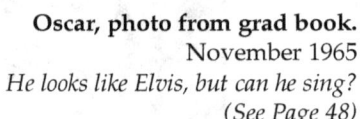

Oscar, photo from grad book.
November 1965
He looks like Elvis, but can he sing?
(See Page 48)

Oscar with future brother-in-law Vinny and Sister-in-law Marylou
December, 1965
Tough kid grad on leave.
(See Page 47)

PHOTOS

Oscar with T-15 survey instrument
February, 1966
If you look closely you can still see the dog.
(See Page 54)

Oscar and Sue, Ramersdorf apartment
October, 1966
Wunderbar!
(See Page 89)

Sue and Snooky, showing Oscar's awards
Christmas, 1966
The best Christmas present I ever got.
(See Page 108)

"Range Rangers" Oscar, Murphy, Bayer, Petty
Spring, 1967
The "ghosting out" crew!
(See Page 119)

Range Rangers Rush, Murphy, and Petty.
Spring 1967
"I'm just f-ing bad."
(See Page 139)

Carmelk with live round.
Graf, Fall 1967
"Look what I found!"
(See Page 123)

"Honest John" firing
Graf, Fall, 1967
"I shot an arrow in the air . . ."
(See Page 111)

www.ingramcontent.com/pod-product-compliance
Lightning Source LLC
Chambersburg PA
CBHW070602010526
44118CB00012B/1425